WHERE
JOY &
Sorrow
Meet

A Way of the Cross

Nicholas Ayo, James Flanigan,
Joseph Ross, J. Massyngbaerde Ford

ave maria press   Notre Dame, Indiana

© 1999 by Ave Maria Press, Inc.
International Standard Book Number: 0-87793-668-4
Cover design by Brian C. Conley
Printed and bound in the United States of America.

Library of Congress Cataloging-in-Publication Data
Where joy and sorrow meet : a way of the cross / Nicholas Ayo . . .
    [et al.].
        p.   cm.
    Includes bibliographical references.
    ISBN 0-87793-668-4
    1. Stations of the Cross.   I. Ayo, Nicholas.
BX2040.W47   1999
232.96—dc21

                                                                    98-37489
                                                                        CIP

*To the family of the
University of Notre Dame*

Contributors

*General introduction and prose meditations
by Nicholas Ayo, C.S.C.*

*Bas-relief stations of the cross
by James Flanigan, C.S.C. Photos by Steve Moriarty.*

Poems for Stations One to Fourteen by Joseph Ross, C.S.C.

Poem for Station Fifteen by Nicholas Ayo, C.S.C.

Orations and intercessions by J. Massyngbaerde Ford.

The artwork in Where Joy and Sorrow Meet *gains a unique, contemporary feel because it is composed of "found" images. Fr. Flanigan drew from photographs of war, crisis, and celebration, including such scenes as firefighters rescuing a victim and an Olympian exulting at his success.*

Contents

Acknowledgments

This publication of the stations of the cross was inspired by a lenten devotion of the graduate students at the University of Notre Dame. I had not prayed the stations of the cross for many years. On that evening in the spring of 1996, I was moved in the depths of my soul. Somewhat later, it seemed that I was being called from within myself to write about this devotional practice.

I began by composing a meditation for each station of the cross. Next, I added an introduction that reflected upon the history and the composition of this ancient devotion in the church. And yet, something was missing. Much more about the stations of the cross might be said in poetry, might be shown in art, might be prayed with compassion.

Fr. James Flanigan, C.S.C., had already sculpted stations of the cross that I greatly admired. I asked if he would allow his work to be included, and he willingly gave photographs by Stephen Moriarty that beautifully captured his art. I then turned to Fr. Joseph Ross, C.S.C., who has been writing powerful poetry in recent years. He agreed to compose a series of fourteen poems for the stations. Finally, I asked Professor J. Massyngbaerde Ford to compose prayers for each station. Josephine Ford is a biblical scholar by profession, but I also know her as a woman of faith who is graced with a genuine and articulate spiritual life. From these contributions the book now before you took birth. Without my collaborators there would have been no book as you now see it, and indeed we are all coauthors of this publication.

I wish to thank Sister Patricia Clark, S.V.M., and Kristin Sadie, a Master of Divinity student at Notre Dame, who brought me back to the devotion of the stations of the cross. Dolores Frese of the English department gave me a poem out of the abundance of her own poetic and spiritual life that I have gratefully included. Macrina Wiederkehr, O.S.B., Sue Pusztai, and Gregory Green, C.S.C., were supportive in ways they may not even know when the work was going slowly. Mary Catherine Rowland helped me sustain my hope for this work. She located beautiful paintings of the stations of the cross by Erica Grimm-Vance, which are found in Holy Child Roman Catholic Church, Regina, Saskatchewan, Canada. Fr. Joseph Balzer, the pastor of the parish, was a gracious host and guide on my visit there. Madonna House in Regina and in Gravelbourg nearby gave me hospitality. Jo Anne DeGidio assisted me with many different versions of the stations of the cross in her own collection.

As my student assistant, Laura Zawadski commented upon and proofread the text. Her willing spirit and high-quality work are much appreciated. Robert Hamma of Ave Maria Press believed in the overall composition and championed its publication. Holly

Taylor Coolman of Ave Maria Press turned an imperfect typescript into an attractive book.

Without all these friends and collaborators there would be no finished product. I cannot tell them and others not mentioned by name how dependent I am upon their assistance and how grateful I am for their involvement. Without them these stations of the cross, now available to others unknown to us all, would never have been at all.

Introduction

"For those who love God, all things commingle unto good" (Rm 8:28). Sorrow and love are two sides of the same coin. Love entails sorrow because we must die, and before we die there are many little deaths in the misunderstandings and separations and offenses of the human condition. Sorrow hides love that has not yet been given eternal life. When sorrow is borne up in hope that the fullness of life will be given, sorrow turns into joy. Sorrow reveals the great love that abides in us. God is love, and Jesus, the beloved son of God, was a man of sorrows. The stations of the cross allow us to walk along with him on the human road of sorrowful love and loving sorrow. "For those who love God, all things commingle unto good."

When someone we love dies in our absence, we want to stand and mourn them in the very place where they suffered and died. We want to visit the scene of the dying, the place where sorrow befell us. Thus it is not surprising that devout Christians have made pilgrimage to the Holy Land, where Jesus was born, and especially to Jerusalem where he shed his blood on the cross. They came to mourn him. They came to pray and to be conformed to him who once walked these streets, but who now lives in the hearts of all people wherever on earth they dwell.

The holiest places in that holy land were named in the gospel narratives. Some other places, such as the house of Veronica, were singled out by tradition. By no means were all these holy places guaranteed to be historically verifiable. Landscapes change, centuries of building and rebuilding destroy the past, memories falter, and mistaken locations take on, over time, a life of their own. The pilgrims came to the holy places, however, not so much to stand at the very spot where Jesus was born or where Jesus died, but more to stand by him in his human suffering. They came to see Jesus, but more with the eye of the soul than with the eye of the body. It was in the end a pilgrimage of the heart more than of the feet.

Not everyone who wished to travel to the Holy Land was able to do so. It was an arduous journey by sea or by land. Great expense was involved, and some risk. Muslims came to rule over the Holy Land in 637, and despite the atrocities and cruelties of the Crusades, retained control over it throughout the Middle Ages. Any public expression of Christian piety in the Holy Land could earn pilgrims scorn and ridicule from the local inhabitants.

The Church of the Holy Sepulcher, built over the traditional place of the crucifixion and burial of Jesus, was considered the most sacred of places. Burned to the ground in 937, the Church of the Holy Sepulcher was rebuilt by the Crusaders, but pilgrims during the Middle Ages often found that they were required to be locked up in the church for the whole night. They were turned out at dawn but were then permitted only guided and limited tours of the Holy Land.

Over the years, pilgrims traced the path backward from the Church of the Holy Sepulcher to Pilate's judgment seat. Following the way of the cross was not immediately envisioned in this practice of visiting the holy places mentioned in the gospel, but the custom of walking the road toward Calvary on the Fridays gradually became a popular devotion cultivated by the Franciscans during the Middle Ages and thereafter. Because so much has changed in the topography of Jerusalem, the way of the cross, or the via sacra (the sacred way), is only an approximation. Where it all ended on Calvary, however, seems rooted in the oldest and best tradition.

The practice of the stations of the cross provided a substitute way to make a pilgrimage to the Holy Land. In one's own church, one could follow the way of the cross. By walking from station to station one might enter into the real presence of Jesus in his passion, without needing to walk the very streets of Palestine. Those unable to travel abroad because of health, lack of wealth, or other obligations would not be left without a heartfelt devotion. Just as the rosary was a way for the illiterate Christian to substitute one hundred and fifty Aves (the Hail Mary prayer) for the psalms of the same number in the Divine Office of the Church, so the stations were a way for the ordinary Christian to follow the way of the cross.

It was in the sixteenth century that the devotion to the fourteen traditional stations was established. The selection and arrangement, however, was not made on site in Jerusalem, but rather in Louvain in Flanders. Jan Van Paeschen, commonly known as Jan Pascha, a Carmelite monk from Mechlin, is given credit for the stations of the cross as we now know them. His work titled Gheestelyck Pelgimagie (Spiritual Pilgrimage) was further solidified and publicized in Europe by the popularity of Jerusalem Sicut Christi Tempore Floruit (Jerusalem as It Stood in the Time of Christ) , which was written in 1584 by Christiaan Van Adrichen, commonly known as Adrichomius. Neither Jan Pascha nor Adrichomius knew the topography or the traditional holy places of Jerusalem directly, but they were devout in their desire to follow the way of the cross in spirit. The details and their historical accuracy were not thought to be a great matter. The person who wished to walk with Jesus did not need exact facts. The general pattern of the gospel passion story, arranged along a devotional way of the cross, would suffice. Empathy for the suffering of Jesus was encouraged. Faith in the cross as the instrument of salvation for all the world was enkindled.

The stations of the cross as arranged by Jan Pascha in Louvain were subsequently imported into Jerusalem. Those who were authorities concerning the holy places, especially the Franciscan scholars, part of the Franciscan Order's long-standing mission from the Vatican to tend the holy places in Jerusalem, knew more of historical fact than did Pascha. And yet, despite much variety in the stations of the cross throughout several centuries, the fourteen stations of Pascha grew so popular among the faithful of western Europe that the Franciscans themselves in Jerusalem began to adopt this form of the via crucis (way of the cross).[1]

The devotion to the stations of the cross spread widely in the years that followed, and eventually hardly a Catholic church in Europe could be found without a representation of the stations. In 1696 Pope Innocent XI granted the Franciscans the faculty to erect stations in their own churches and to bestow special indulgences. In 1731 Pope Clement XII allowed the stations to be erected outside of Franciscan churches, and he attached the same indulgences as would be received in Jerusalem itself. For the stations to be erected in a church nothing more was needed than fourteen small wooden crosses and a blessing ceremony by a priest deputized by the Franciscan Order. Many churches mounted elaborate pictorial representations of the stations, whether in painting, engraving, or sculpture. The stations of the cross as we know them today are the product of a long development in which the details of history were mingled with piety and devotion and in turn interpreted by artistry of every kind.

In the traditional fourteen stations, seven episodes are clearly gospel narrative, and they are the central events of the stations of the cross. Stations Ten to Fourteen would hardly be disputed by anyone, and these five stations make a balanced drama of the crucifixion itself. Jesus is stripped naked of his clothes (10), nailed to a cross (11), hung alive to die (12), unnailed dead from the cross (13), and clothed in a shroud for burial (14). The first two stations seem equally without question. Jesus is condemned by Pontius Pilate (1) to carry his cross (2) and be crucified, a fact central even to the ancient Apostles' creed: "suffered under Pontius Pilate, was crucified, died, and was buried."

What is peculiar about the fourteen stations is the role of two women and the account of three falls of Jesus. That Jesus met his mother (4) is plausible enough, if Mary was present at the foot of the cross as John's gospel reports (19:25). Veronica wiping the face of Jesus (6) seems to be an invention of popular devotion, perhaps included only as far back as the late Middle Ages. This woman who appears from nowhere and takes away the only portrait of the face of Jesus ever known may represent the human need for a relic of the beloved, a need which has also kept alive the hope that the shroud of Turin gives us an authentic touch of the flesh and bones of Jesus. The fourth station when Mary meets Jesus and the fifth station when Veronica wipes the face of Jesus with a cloth would seem plausible extensions of the gospel witness that it was the women who followed Jesus on the way of the cross. The daughters of Jerusalem consoling Jesus (8) is mentioned at length in the gospel (Lk 23:27-31). These three stations (4, 6, 8) feminize the story even more strongly than the gospel narratives which record only that the women are present at the crucifixion scene and they look on from a distance. The compassion of these women is the only kindness that Jesus receives from Pilate's judgment seat to Calvary hill. Even before his condemnation, Pilate's wife proclaims the innocence of Jesus, because of her dream about him. In the passion story it is women who are presented as loving and life-caring. The men are death-dealing. The male disciples of Jesus all run away, Peter thrice denies the man, and the young man in Mark so thoroughly abandons Jesus that he runs off without his clothes (Mk 14:52).

The three falls of Jesus carrying his cross have no mention in the gospels, though such suffering is plausible. There is a suggestion, for example, that Jesus is faltering in the gospel account of Simon of Cyrene (5) being impressed to help Jesus carry his cross. Clearly Jesus was weakening, and there was fear that he would either die before he was crucified or that he would move so slowly that the crucifixion would not be done with by sundown of the sabbath. If Jesus was thus failing, he was probably also falling. These multiple falls surely dramatize the way of the cross and add poignancy. Every human being stumbles, and when burdens are too heavy we often fall. The strength and courage to rise from our falls reveal our character, and indeed the falls of Jesus on the via crucis might be seen as a foreshadowing of his great fall into the tomb and his great rising from the depths of death itself.

Let us examine more closely the three falls of Jesus on the way to Calvary. Why does it appeal to popular devotion that Jesus falls more than once? Why do the stations have three falls that are scarcely differentiated? One may presume that each fall was more terrible and debilitating and that the injuries were cumulative. Even so, the falls seem repetitious. Perhaps more than one fall was needed for us to believe that the first fall was not just an accident. It is when we fall a second time that we recognize with some terror that our trouble might become a repeated one and our falls more than we can avoid. Once is surprise; two is an alarm. Three times, and we fear there is a pattern and a dire prediction of how the unavoidable pain in our future will unfold.

Stations Three to Nine comprise Jesus' walk to Golgotha and the carrying of his cross. That walk begins with a fall and ends with a fall. Those seven stations (3-9), only slightly developed in the biblical accounts, show the most creativity in the imagination of the faithful, whose piety strove to identify the contemporary Christian with the suffering Jesus of yesterday. The seven stations that comprise this difficult journey are made up of three falls and the several people (Simon of Cyrene and the women) whose love touches Jesus in his sorrowful walk to his death. These two contrasting themes do have some biblical warrant, as we have seen. The Simon of Cyrene account gives plausibility to the falls, and the daughters of Jerusalem in the gospel story give plausibility to the intervention of Mary and of Veronica.

These seven stations present an alternation of consolation and desolation. Jesus is either buoyed up or thrown down. Here is the human condition. Here is the Christian life, where joy and sorrow mingle, where hope and discouragement crisscross. Jesus is consoled in some fashion four times (4, 5, 6, 8), and he is driven down in the falls to the ground three times (3, 7, 9). The desolations are intermingled among the consolations. That suffering body of Jesus lives on in all human beings whose life of necessity comprises a way of the cross, with ups and downs, lived in the hope that one might pass from agony to glory in the mystery of the cross of Jesus Christ. Our human lifetime is thus conformed to the cross in the pattern of Good Friday. We must all carry our cross.

One could more precisely define the way of the cross as that period of time and space when the body of Jesus is in contact with the wood of the cross. In the fourteen stations, the condemnation of Jesus (1) is prologue, and the burial of Jesus (14) is epilogue. That's how it begins; that's how it ends. From Station Two when Jesus accepts the wood of the cross to Station Thirteen when Jesus is unfastened from the cross he embraced in the beginning, his body is in intimate contact with the wood of the cross. The crucifixion, of course, is the climax of the stations of the cross. The three stations that detail the crucifixion itself depict the scene in agonizing slow motion, a scene well attested in the gospel passion narratives. Jesus is no longer walking. Jesus is stripped of his clothes (10), nailed to his cross (11), and hung in the sight of the public to die (12).

III Few human beings are asked to walk to their death. It is those who are put to death who must walk to their death, whether in greatest pain as in crucifixion or as painless as possible in lethal injection. In any case, it is an awful walk, the walk of the dead. The condemned is literally a "dead man walking," and only those who care greatly will walk with the living dead. Such is the way of cross; such are the stations of the cross. We walk with Jesus in his agony.

Our whole life is a walk on the road of life, a journey through time and space, a passage from this life to eternal life. Human life is a pilgrim's way to the city of God. In Luke's gospel Jesus' whole life is centered upon his long journey up to Jerusalem where he would die. It is the way to God. Jesus said he was "the way, and the truth, and the life" (Jn 14:6). To be a Christian, to be a follower of Jesus Christ, it is not enough to talk the talk. We must all walk the walk that is the way of the cross. We must carry our cross and follow our Lord. "If any want to become my followers, let them deny themselves and take up their cross daily and follow me. For those who want to save their life will lose it, and those who lose their life for my sake will save it. What does it profit them if they gain the whole world, but lose or forfeit themselves?" (Lk 9:23-25) The stations of the cross are a reminder of this ever-present paschal mystery. It is in dying that we are born to eternal life. The stations are a remembrance of what Jesus suffered for love of us. The stations are a rehearsal so that we walk in his footsteps: "Choosing compassion: the love that suffers. Attempting to lift/eliminate the burdens and sorrows of the world. Falling, again and again. Knowing you can't go it alone. Standing in solidarity with your fellow suffering humans. Taking the way of Jesus to God" (McAnally).

On the road to Calvary, Christian devotion has chosen fourteen stations, or snapshots, in the passion of Jesus. It is as if we are asked to stand there a moment and become part of his suffering. The word "station" is derived from the Latin word "to stand," and indeed the stations of the cross invite one to take a stand in the spiritual life. In the Roman military a station was an outpost, a guard duty in the night, a place to watch and to wait, keeping alert to danger and ready to respond. Taking one's station might properly be related to the military cry of "battle stations!" With whom does one stand? Listen to the hymn about Mary, the mother of Jesus: "At the cross her station keeping, stood the mournful mother weeping." We are each and all part of the passion story of Jesus, and we have our station.

The bad news is in our newspapers, but the good news is in the gospel narratives of the suffering, death, and resurrection of Jesus. The stations of the cross remind us that death is changed to life, because of the power of love that transforms everything about the human condition. "There is never love without sorrow, never commitment without pain, never involvement without loss, never giving without suffering" (Nouwen). Where there was despair, now there is hope. Where there was sorrow, now there is joy.

Jesus Is
Sentenced to Die

Jesus is in the foreground, standing tall, up front, all alone, made an object by the scene in all its implications. He is the one who is blindfolded, though it is Justice that is supposed to be blindfolded and impartial. Jesus' hands are tied in front of him. Behind him the perspective leads one into the endless corridors of power only to disappear. Jesus is powerless. Ecce homo *(Here is the man!).*

To the side and bottom is a prison window grill; a face peers out from within yet imprisoned. Human beings are caged behind bars in a jail; they are held as animals. All the issues of crime and the punishment of the innocent-yet-unwanted also rise up from this scene.

> Blessed are those who are persecuted for righteousness' sake,
> for theirs is the kingdom of heaven.
> ——Matthew 5:10

"'Shall I crucify your King?' . . . 'We have no king but the emperor.' Then he handed him over to them to be crucified" (Jn 19:15-16). There is no justice in this world, though there is mercy, for "where sin increased, grace abounded all the more" (Rm 5:20). Into this, our human condition, Jesus stood among us. He was flogged and tortured, and then in a pitiable condition he was presented to the angry crowd crying out for his death. "Here is the man!" (Jn 19:5). Behold the human condition! Yet suffering brought Jesus no pity. What would be, would be. "Crucify him, crucify him!" And Pontius Pilate, the Roman Procurator, washed his hands of Jesus, "meek and humble of heart," though these blood stains would never come out.

Willful human blindness put Jesus to death. We are afraid of the truth because we are afraid of our life. We are afraid of our life because we are afraid of our death. "The verdict first and then the evidence," says the queen in *Alice in Wonderland*. We have our hearts set on self-protection, and so we allow the truth to be obscured and justice to be undone. We know what we want, and so we want no interference from what we do not know. Jesus said he was a king, but his kingdom was one of truth. And Pilate said in the dark sinfulness of the human heart, "What is truth?" (Jn 18:38). In colloquial speech, "I am all I've got, and I don't want to get involved." After all, "Am I my brother's keeper?" (Gen 4:9). Then Jesus is silent. The just man is speechless. The Word of God, the Lord of all who will come "to judge the living and the dead," stands mute under human judgment. In so many ways, so many places, so many times, human beings have no choice about what will be.

To be human is thus to bear the cross. We are all sentenced to death when we are born. "Ask not for whom the bell tolls, it tolls for thee." We are all sentenced to life when we are born. Like it or not our body is imposed on us, whether male or female, whether healthy or sick, in this time and place and in no other. We are given all the genetic joys and sorrows of our forebears, and we are handed over every day to chance and accident, "the slings and arrows of outrageous fortune." It is the human condition. Life is not fair, though in God's providence it proves to be gracious. The philosopher Hegel writes, "History is a butcher's block."

And yet "consider the lilies, how they grow: they neither toil nor spin; yet I tell you, even Solomon in all his glory was not clothed like one of these. But if God so clothes the grass of the field, which is alive today and tomorrow is thrown into the oven, how much more will he clothe you—you of little faith!" (Lk 12:27-28) To be human is to stand in our flesh before God, whose ways are not our ways. In the cross of Jesus Christ we find our only hope.

Note

Jesus' condemnation to death has received various possible explanations: (1) It was God's will, his Father's will, an atonement for sin required by divine justice. (2) He fell into the hands of wicked men. (3) The Jewish religious establishment was scandalized by his statements, such as "before Abraham was, I am" (Jn 8:58), and they accused him of blasphemy worthy of death. (4) Religious leaders were envious of his popularity, for they admitted "if we let him go on like this, everyone will believe in him" (Jn 11:48). (5) Pontius Pilate was convinced Jesus might be perceived as a king who threatened Roman dominion. He agreed with the Jewish leaders that it was "better for you to have one man die for the people than to have the whole nation destroyed" (Jn 11:50). (6) Judas betrayed him, not so much out of callous feeling, but rather to force the hand of Jesus to resist the status quo. If arrested, Jesus would have to use his power to break free, and thereby a new political day would be born. (7) Jesus was a troublemaker with his critique of the status quo. For human beings, "might is right," and thus Jesus was a revolutionary in his demonstration that God does not abuse others as those in power always do. Unconditional love is upsetting, and thus Jesus had to be put to death. In short, Jesus died because equality, mutuality, and unconditional acceptance are radically subversive of any human system of oppression, Jewish or Roman, then or now. Jesus was a friend of the poor and of sinners, of tax collectors and of prostitutes, and thus no friend of the law that exploited all these people and kept them in their place.

God the Father required no pound of flesh in expiation of our sins. One might conclude that Jesus died because of the persistence of his love that would tell the truth even if those Jesus tried to love perceived the truth of God's love as a threat to their welfare in this sinful world. As a wounded and frightened animal will bite the hand that comes to heal it, so humanity bit the hand of God, killing the lamb of God, in whose blood we all have been washed clean at the last.

The looming judge
spat out the words:
"Sentenced to death."

I heard nothing else.
As if underwater.
Everything fogged, distorted:
wiggling and waving
in watery white shock.

Out the corner of my eye
I saw a crowd cheering.
Then my head was dunked
underwater again.
Water in my ears,
in my nose,
in my mouth,
in my eyes.
Nothing to say or see or feel or know
except what they do
to me.

Hands chained to waist,
ankle chained to ankle,
hope is flood-chased
from the debacle
that is me.

My eyes rise
just above water's line:
"What have I done?"
For a fraction of fury
this?"

The crowing judge spits at me again.
"Do you understand what I said, boy?"
His white hands shove my head under again.
All water,
all rushing
I totter
toward the crushing
that is me.

Prayer

Sevenfold Spirit,
    as we walk these stations
        speak to us in your still small voice.
            May some new understanding
                pervade our hearts. Amen.

Gracious God, our Father and our Mother,
    you are not impassable, immovable, devoid of emotion.
You experience infinite anguish
    over the waywardness and brutality of your people.
Here we stand. We desire to be one with
    your Son and our brother, Jesus.
We are seared by the scorching scorn of Pilate,
    "Behold, Humanity!" and "What is Truth?"
By the silence and gentleness of your Son
    enable us to pass the death sentence
on anger and war
    on lust and lechery
        on deceit and sloth
            on arrogance and tyranny
            on selfishness
                on all that effaces
                    your divine image and likeness.
            Amen.

Intercessions

Response: Christ, true disciple, hear us.

For unjust judges:
   Christ, true disciple, hear us.

For those on death row:
   Christ, true disciple, hear us.

For those floundering in the baptism of suffering:
   Christ, true disciple, hear us.

For the wisdom of silence:
   Christ, true disciple, hear us.

For the gift of hope hidden in the fertile soil of sorrow:
   Christ, true disciple, hear us.

Jesus Receives His Cross

The cross is overwhelming, too large to carry. Jesus totters on his feet. He seems almost to embrace the wood, this instrument of death. The whole cross hangs over him, both the beam and the crossbeam. His knees are buckling, but his first steps all alone are full of a stark courage. Stations One and Two are related, since the condemnatory verdict is then executed by Jesus receiving his cross and starting out to Calvary. The artist depicts them both in one panel. In the background are the balanced and supporting arches of the palaces of justice, which form an ironic commentary on the whole scene. Jesus moves alone into the light that lies ahead of him, though the cross looms above him and overshadows him.

Blessed are the pure in heart, for they will see God.
——Matthew 5:8

Tell me the decisions of your lifetime and the choices of your heart, and I will tell you who you are. Jesus made the costliest of choices: to die for love of us. He was not obliged to die; we are constrained to die because of our sins. Jesus accepted lovingly our death even to the cross to save us from the impact of our sins. "No one takes it [my life] from me, but I lay it down of my own accord. I have power to lay it down, and I have power to take it up again" (Jn 10:18). Dying in such agony was a willing decision of divine and human love. "Now my soul is troubled. And what should I say—'Father, save me from this hour'? No, it is for this reason that I have come to this hour. Father, glorify your name" (Jn 12:27-28). Jesus receives his cross as the chosen last and ultimate way to manifest his love for us without limits. "No one has greater love than this, to lay down one's life for one's friends (Jn 15:13).

Jesus deliberately carried the wood of his own sacrifice to the altar, just as Isaac carried the wood when Abraham led his son up the mountain as the lamb of sacrifice (Gen 22:6). Jesus carrying his cross "is the Lamb of God who takes away the sin of the world" (Jn 1:29). Here as well is the "lion of Judah," who does not return evil for evil, but who absorbs the darkness in the promise of a new earth and a new heaven.

36

Because of this wood on those vulnerable shoulders, "the wolf shall live with the lamb, the leopard shall lie down with the kid, the calf and the lion and the fatling together, and a little child shall lead them" (Is 11:6). Gone is the imagined God of power who wants human sacrifice and whom humanity always feared; come is the God of love who was born a baby in a stable and died on a cross saying, "Father, forgive them; for they do not know what they are doing" (Lk 23:34).

Our life with all its givens, good and bad crisscrossed, and with inevitable and unwanted death, can be either accepted in hope or rejected in despair. All our days commingle to form in us a yes or a no to the ways of God. "If any want to become my followers, let them deny themselves and take up their cross and follow me. For those who want to save their life will lose it, and those who lose their life for my sake will find it" (Mt 16:24-25). We can be grateful for the mystery of this, our life, in our world where God is most hidden, or we can be resentful. Our attitude is always ours to claim. Human beings are about as willing as they choose to be. We can carry our cross that burdens our life and our death, or we can drag it along. Jesus receives his cross with a kiss, for it was his Father's cross, and it must conceal within its hard injustice the soft mercy of a Father's love for his only son. Ave crux, spes unica! Welcome to the cross, our only hope! "A disciple is not above the teacher, nor a slave above the master" (Mt 10:24). Jesus receives his cross as a moment from God and as the unique way given him to love to the end us who are his friends. "So they took Jesus; and carrying the cross by himself, he went out to what is called *The Place of the Skull*" (Jn 19:16-17).

Note

Why the condemned criminal was compelled to carry the wood for his own execution to the place of crucifixion is not evident. Perhaps the procession of the suffering and doomed man through the crowded streets of the city was meant as an example to others who might defy Roman law. Perhaps carrying the wood of the cross was intended to wear out the victim and hasten his death after crucifixion. We do not know if the vertical wooden beam was permanently in place and therefore the condemned man carried only the crossbeam. In Christian art, however, Jesus has been most often depicted carrying both arms of the cross. And so it might have been.

It's like digging your own grave.
You make your bed, you lie in it.
Your own deeds greet you,
every second of every minute
of every hour of every day.

You hug the wood for dear life,
or hug nothing for dear death.
Every strife, every breath
bears a beam sliver-full,
anxious to form
against your arm.

A rough-grained shadow
lumbers toward you:
"Try me on,
'til all your days devote
their knotted passing
to me alone."

"Carry me. I'll lead you."
This tree will not bend,
this wood will not lend
you one damn cent.

"Carry me. I'll lead you."
Like lover carries lover
to the gas chamber.

It's the final bed,
a moment's dread,
this tempting tree
saying:
"Carry me."

Prayer

Blessed Trinity, you are
    the pliant branches of the Holy Tree,
the still, small groan in the healing leaves of the Spirit.
    By mutual consent, you accepted a gross and torturous death,
the infamous gibbet, the accursed tree,
    punishment for the crime of the world.
By your Spirit, promised to all who bear
    a martyr's witness to their faith,
tutor us to be
    rooted in your love,
bending gracefully to your will,
    reaching up, up to your light.
                             Amen.

Intercessions

Response: Christ, tree of life, hear us.

For all those in prisons, camps, or torture chambers:
    Christ, tree of life, hear us.

For the underprivileged and the dehumanized:
    Christ, tree of life, hear us.

For the overprivileged and the indifferent:
    Christ, tree of life, hear us.

For holy discretion in the decisions of life:
    Christ, tree of life, hear us.

Jesus Falls the First Time

III

Jesus seems more to falter than to fall. He seems hardly able to stand up or to lift up the weight of the cross. He catches himself and he catches the cross before it falls to the ground, but his upright stance is quite broken. In the second fall, Jesus will be kneeling and straddling the cross, while Simon tries to talk him into taking up the cross again. In the third fall, Jesus is flat on his back, and the cross is pressed into the ground. He is ready to be nailed down. Dead tired, dead on his feet, now he seems dead on his back. His arms are wide spread and his legs open. No Simon is in sight and no help.

Stations Three and Four are yoked together by the artist. If the soldiers are now looking for a Simon to assist Jesus and the procession has come to a halt, then it was a moment for his mother Mary to approach Jesus.

> Blessed are the meek, for they will inherit the earth.
> ——Matthew 5:5

We know that Jesus had been cruelly flogged by order of Pilate, and we can assume he was much weakened both by loss of sleep and by loss of blood. Perhaps he had no food to eat nor water to drink. The daytime may have been hot, and suffering in shock from his torments, Jesus could have been dizzy or exhausted. He may have been prodded to move faster despite the weight of the cross. In the passion narratives, Simon of Cyrene is compelled by the Roman soldiers to assist Jesus, who must have been failing and probably falling. Christian imagination senses how heavy the cross really weighed for Jesus. The sins of the world crushed him. If Jesus shared our human condition, Jesus shared our burden and felt our collapse. "But I was like a gentle lamb led to the slaughter. And I did not know it was against me that they devised schemes saying, 'Let us destroy the tree with its fruit, let us cut him off from the land of the living, so that his name will no longer be remembered!'" (Jer 11:19)

Gravity brings Jesus down. He whom no sin ever felled is brought low by the weight of the tree of life. He is cut down by a burden beyond his human strength. Jesus collapses with no one and nothing to hold him up now. He falls because the body is wounded. He falls because our bones break, because our land erodes, because all things must bend, because force is the sovereign of this material world, and because in the end, as the children's song says, "Ashes, ashes, all fall down." Children whose shoelaces break in their hands know in their souls that they themselves must break, and that everyone they love will someday fall apart. And we all know that "the ring of roses of good names and humble hopes all fall down, beaten, whipped, shot, all fall down" (De Vinck). Jesus must have known with desperation as the ground rose to meet his falling down that he was altogether human and that he was indeed about to die. Human beings are mortal life, fragile flesh, vulnerable bodies. In our sinfulness we also know a fall from grace and our first loss of innocence. Jesus on the ground is one of us in his unprotected weakness and human like us to the core of his sinless being. He cannot stand up, and none of us stands up for long. "The text being written in the dailiness of newspapers hardly knows anything but the shape of the fallen" (De Vinck). "God writes straight with crooked lines," says a Portuguese proverb. God walks straight with fallings down. Jesus becomes a wounded healer, and "by his wounds you have been healed" (1 Pt 2:24).

Note

In the traditional stations of the cross, Jesus falls soon after receiving the cross. There is no mention of such a fall in the passion narratives of the gospels, though it may be implied in the assistance compelled of Simon of Cyrene in the carrying of the cross. It is quite possible that Stations Three, Four, Five, and Six are all one slow motion. Because Jesus falls, his mother has a time to speak to him as he rises to his feet. Then the soldiers impress Simon to help Jesus carry the cross. Before the procession is ready to begin again, with Simon lifting the cross behind Jesus, Veronica has a chance to emerge from the crowd and wipe his face.

Gravel rolls foot onto ankle,
which drops knee to road
in a skin-scraping pound.

Balance turns to gray-black blur
'til crowds and cries and cross
kick into an open-eyed cartwheel.

Thigh rakes wood.
Splinters scratch skin.
Against his will,
he greets gravity
and falls.

Prayer

Incarnate God, like the Israelites in Egypt,
    you begin your Exodus.
You jostle through the straightened lanes of Jerusalem,
    bustling, busy with Passover fare.
We lament the inhumanity of humankind,
    the ribald humor and obscene gestures
escorting a prisoner's faltering struggle along death row.
    Grant us grace to distance ourselves
from the capricious, importunate masses
    and to stand face-to-face with the wounded
        as friend to Friend.
                Amen.

Intercessions

Response: Jesus, mocked and fallible, hear us.

For all who, like the Israelites, flee from conditions of oppression:
    Jesus, mocked and fallible, hear us.

For those who find the cross of Jesus to be a stumbling block or folly:
    Jesus, mocked and fallible, hear us.

For the obliteration of all cruel laughter:
    Jesus, mocked and fallible, hear us.

For healing for those suffering from the nightmare of war experiences:
    Jesus, mocked and fallible, hear us.

For the grace to resist the influence of the crowd:
    Jesus, mocked and fallible, hear us.

Jesus Encounters His Mother Mary

Just Jesus and Mary are depicted by the artist. She is on her feet and whispers closely in his ear, and he turns his face to her. The cross is not visible between them or even around them. They are alone, mother and son, surrounded by the sorrows of the world and enfolded in the intimacy of their good-bye.

> Blessed are those who mourn, for they will be comforted.
> ——Matthew 5:4

He was a "man of suffering and acquainted with infirmity" (Is 53:3), and she was a woman of sorrows. All you who pass by, "Look and see if there is any sorrow like my sorrow" (Lam 1:12). He was the "son of man," the "suffering servant." She was the sorrowful mother, the mater dolorosa, to whom Simeon had foretold: "This child is destined for the falling and the rising of many in Israel, and to be a sign that will be opposed so that the inner thoughts of many will be revealed—and a sword will pierce your own soul too" (Lk 2:34-35). Jesus was born to die for the salvation of the world. Mary's heart was pierced with sorrow at the time of his passion and death. His heart was pierced at the end of his life as he hung on the cross, for he died to give birth to a people of God. "One of the soldiers pierced his side with a spear, and at once blood and water came out" (Jn 19:34). Jesus had been a baby in her arms, and now at the hour of his death he was yet her child. "Can a woman forget her nursing child, or show no compassion for the child of her womb? Even these may forget, yet I will not forget you" (Is 49:15).

When Mary's body bled on straw
To first reveal the sacred face,
Her mortal flesh upheld the law
Of kind, and newly saving grace
Whereby was kept the death of god.
The head of Jesus, crowned with hay,
Came between beasts where Mary lay.

When Mary's body anguished drew,
Her bended knees nor wordless sound
Did neither pray exemption there,
But cried so clear the shining ground
Of all that worthy is, and good.

And surely Mary's body bled,
For Jesus' blood was surely shed.

—Dolores Frese

To the widow of Naim Jesus restored her only son, who was being carried out for burial (Lk 7:11-17). Now the only son of God encounters his widowed mother as he is being led out to his own death. Jesus and Mary say to each other what all human beings must say when we make our last farewell and adieu. Forgive me! Forgive me the further pain I must cause you by knowing that I am suffering alongside of you. I would gladly take your place, suffer your pain, and die your death. I also am the burden you must bear. I am not able to love you as I would. I ask your forgiveness and altogether give you mine. And then they must have said with their eyes an immense thank-you for all that had been, for all that was even now in agony, and for all God was doing to bring about the triumph of love despite the ravages of sin and death. One can imagine through hopeful tears the outpouring of the last words, "I love you," that enfolds sorrow and grief in farewell. Such a simple good-bye (god-be-with-you) must have been said somehow and somewhere by mother and by son.

Note

The meeting of Jesus with his mother along the way of the cross seems so right and just. Surely Mary stood by her son, whatever anyone else may have failed to do. We are not sure whether Mary had come up to Jerusalem for this Passover celebration. There is no indication that she was an habitual member of the entourage that followed Jesus in his itinerant preaching. We do know that she must have been nearby; there would not have been enough time to send a message to Nazareth after the arrest of Jesus to allow her time to come up to Jerusalem before his death. We know that Jesus and Mary must have had their farewell, but exactly where and when may not be known for certain. The inner communion of Jesus and Mary must have transcended time and space as we know it. We do know that Jesus encountered a group of women mourners as he carried the cross on the way to Calvary (Lk 23:27-31). It is quite plausible that Mary would have been among these women or among the crowd following Jesus to Calvary. The fourth station allows our very human imagination to appreciate this final encounter of Jesus and his mother on the way to Calvary with the poignancy that it would arouse in a compassionate soul.

John's gospel puts Mary at the foot of the cross as Jesus dies. It may be the evangelist's arranging a theological statement, for it is not likely that the soldiers allowed anyone to come so close to Jesus. More probably Mary would have waited along the way to Calvary to see him pass, to speak to him in the narrow street, and then to follow the soldiers leading Jesus to Calvary. We have no mention in the other three gospels that Mary was present at his crucifixion, even though they mention by name several women less known in the life of Jesus. "There were also women looking on from a distance; among them were Mary Magdalene, and Mary the mother of James the younger and of Joses, and Salome" (Mk 15:40). However, Mary, the mother of Jesus, could no doubt have been overlooked in the crowd and confusion.

She surely saw this coming.
All the enemies,
all the threats,
her own blood
about to be spilled
from him.

They call this a contact visit:
She gets to touch her death row son.
His red prison suit, its stenciled numbers,
her sobbing hair pressed against his still-
    breathing chest.
"It's all right, Mama."
He caresses her cheek tears
with uncuffed hands.

Mary speaks straight to his ear.
Her voice firm as the cross:
"It's all right, son. You walk all the way."
His friends watch her nerve;
theirs long gone.
Her muscled words
harden his knees.

Her tightening throat
breaks the words in half:
"always loved you, always loved you."
He shifts her shoulders
for the first separation.
The chain rattles between his ankles
like the guards' irrelevant keys.

Her graying wisdom
nods him forward.
She straightens herself,
shoulder, back, true:
"I have always loved you.
"I have always loved you."

Prayer

Compassionate God, faithful friend of the oppressed,
    you were the liberator of the Israelites from the brutality of Egypt.

Your Spirit raised up five heroic women,
    Shiphrah and Puah, the wise midwives,
the mother of Moses, his sister, Miriam,
    and Pharaoh's daughter.

You raised up prophetesses, like Deborah and Hulda,
    and women saviors, like Esther and Judith.
Now your Spirit pervades Mary of Nazareth,
    true disciple, sage and mother.
She stands, no "damsel in distress," but stalwart, unflinching,
    like the mother of the seven boy martyrs.[2]
Grant to us, as women and mothers,
    the grace to trust the divine calling of our children.
May we inspire them by our tearless courage
    and by our ardent hope in the resurrection and eternal life.
                  Amen.

Intercessions

Response: Mary, faithful disciple, intercede for us.

For the mothers of the "disappeared":
    Mary, true disciple, intercede for us.

For mothers whose children risk their lives for the truth:
    Mary, true disciple, intercede for us.

For unwed fathers that they may take loving responsibility for their children:
    Mary, true disciple, intercede for us.

For parents overwhelmed with sorrow:
    Mary, true disciple, intercede for us.

For children that they might prudently discern their calling from God:
    Mary, true disciple, intercede for us.

Simon of Cyrene Helps Jesus Carry His Cross

Simon is in the background. His figure is smaller and slighter. He cannot easily take hold of the cross, unless he were to take the whole cross upon himself. Jesus is in the center of the scene. His back is bent, the cross is dragging, and his eyes are turned to the soldier as if waiting a decision. The soldier turns his back to the viewer and dominates the foreground in an impersonal way. He looms large and menacing, no doubt impatient to move forward and to get it all over.

Blessed are the merciful, for they will receive mercy.
——Matthew 5:7

No man is an island. Our lives are entangled for better or for worse at every turn. We lean on one another. We depend on one another. We are responsible for those we love and those we do not love. "Bear one another's burdens, and in this way you will fulfill the law of Christ" (Gal 6:2). Everybody is trouble to somebody. We are all in debt to others before us and around us who support us. It is ever more that we owe than we can repay. Therefore we pray: "Forgive us our debts, as we also have forgiven our debtors" (Mt 6:12).

Do we accept this human exchange of help with gratitude or resentment? "He ain't heavy; he's my brother" the line goes, reminding us that love makes the burden light. Jesus said his yoke was easy and his burden light, and one might think of the yoke of an oxen team pulling side by side. Love given and received doubles our joys and halves our sorrows. We must help each other carry the cross of Jesus now become our own cross. "'Lord, when was it that we saw you hungry and gave you food, or thirsty and gave you something to drink? . . . And when was it that we saw you sick or in prison and visited you?' And the king will answer them, 'Truly I tell you, just as you did it to one of the least of these who are members of my family, you did it to me'" (Mt 25:37-40).

Jesus was failing on the road to Calvary. The soldiers had orders to crucify him before sunset, which marked the beginning of the Passover festival. "They compelled a passer-by, who was coming in from the country, to carry his cross; it was Simon of Cyrene, the father of Alexander and Rufus" (Mk 15:21). "And they laid the cross on him, and made him carry it behind Jesus" (Lk 23:26). So should we follow Jesus in the carrying of his cross. We are either helping to lift the cross or we are imposing the cross on someone else's shoulders. We are either with Jesus or we are against him. Our life is either a yes or a no.

The figures along the way of the cross who touch Jesus in some way represent in a quick sketch the human condition. Our paths crisscross. Life is what happens while we are planning something else. Jesus was an interruption for Simon, just as love is always an interruption of heartfelt giving crossing heartfelt need. We are ever coming to a crossroad. We do not know if Simon reacted to the plight of Jesus as a good Samaritan touched with compassion or whether he carried the cross per force and with reluctance. Even if the latter, perhaps he changed his mind like the centurion when Jesus died, or the good thief crucified beside him.

Note

How and why Simon came to Jerusalem we do not know. Perhaps he was a pilgrim coming to the Temple for the Passover festival. There was a large Jewish population in Cyrene (Acts 2:10 and 6:9), which was in North Africa (today Libya). He was coming in from the countryside when he encountered Jesus, and we are reminded that the place of crucifixion was outside the walls of the city and alongside a busy road. Simon is singled out, perhaps because he was a foreigner and his manner of dress or facial features gave him away. That his name is retained in the passion narratives suggests he may later have become a Christian and was well known. His two sons, Rufus and Alexander, are mentioned by name, and there is a Rufus, who is a Christian, in Paul's letter to the Romans (16:13).

Fresh hands.
Fresh legs.
Fresh shoulders.
All awaiting wood,
ready to feel
the back-biting teeth
of another man's sentence.

Relief and fear collide
and relief wins.
But does it travel with another beating?
"Can he help me?"
"Will you really let him help me?"

Military urgency
allows short-term compassion.
"Hell, yeah. Take it."
It's just soldierly avoidance
of a premature death
that would require an administrative
explanation.

This shouldering
doesn't lend much to sharing.

You'll either let him help me—
or you won't.
You either carry it—
or you don't.

Prayer

Jesus, you bade your disciples
 take up the cross and follow you.
Simon is the first to implement this.
 Blessed be Simon, impressed into service
under a military regime.
 Willingly or unwillingly he shared
your penalty, your pain, your embarrassment
 so that you might bring your mission to perfection.
Be with those in our contemporary society
 who must bow, mortified in body, resilient in soul,
to imperialist and military powers.
 Raise up for them Simons of Justice and Compassion.
           Amen.

Intercessions

Response: Jesus, disdaining not human help, hear us.

For those whose occupation requires them to torture others, may the Spirit of understanding make them revolutionaries of gentleness in their society:
    Jesus, disdaining not human help, hear us.

For those who have jeopardized their reputation in order to help others:
    Jesus, disdaining not human help, hear us.

For the grace and ability to accept assistance:
    Jesus, disdaining not human help, hear us.

For animals subjected to fear and suffering because of human selfishness:
    Jesus, disdaining not human help, hear us.

In thanksgiving for the Simons in our lives:
    Jesus, disdaining not human help, hear us.

Veronica Wipes the Face of Jesus

Veronica is in the foreground and moving away from Jesus. She holds the cloth in her hands, and it is a large piece of fabric. Perhaps she has just discovered the image of the face of Jesus imprinted upon the cloth. Perhaps the cloth itself is a part of her dress, her veil, or some outer piece of apparel such as a shawl. She is alone. Her dress is knee-length, and her hair sways with her motion. Her clothing accentuates the breasts of her feminine figure and its compassionate nature.

> Blessed are the merciful, for they will receive mercy.
> ———Matthew 5:7

Of all the stations, surely the story of Veronica is the most intriguing. She is a figure of mystery, emerging out of the crowd and then disappearing, taking with her the one and only likeness of Jesus miraculously imprinted on the cloth with which she wiped his face. Who was she? Any one of us ought to have stepped forward and rendered this simple kindness to this gentle man helpless in such obvious anguish. But it is told that only Veronica stood up for Jesus with a cloth in her hand and no mind to the consequence.

One should never be a mere spectator to agony. "Random acts of kindness and senseless beauty" confirm our humanity. Veronica is a female Simon, and he a male Veronica. The gesture of compassion required of Simon per force erupted with spontaneity from Veronica. "'Come,' my heart says, 'seek his face!' Your face, Lord, do I seek. Do not hide your face from me" (Ps 27: 8-9). Veronica abandoned the safety of the crowd and took Jesus something of her clothes. She may have torn off her veil or head kerchief, found a napkin or a handkerchief, or allowed Jesus to sink his bleeding face into the folds of her dress. Perhaps he had fallen and she knelt down beside him.

She gave of her clothing; she gave of herself. She wiped the face of Jesus clean, and what had been ugly became beautiful. Compassion is the princess who kisses the frog, the beauty that embraces the beast, the love that is willing to touch pain and passion and turn them into salvation. It is when Veronica covers the disfigured face of Jesus that she discovers the divine face of her Lord and savior.

Legend says that Veronica is thought to be the woman with the hemorrhage who touched the clothes of Jesus. "Who touched my clothes?" asks Jesus (Mk 5:30). "He looked all around to see who had done it. But the woman, knowing what had happened to her, came in fear and trembling, fell down before him, and told him the whole truth" (Mk 5:32-33). The man whose cloth had stopped the woman's bleeding of twelve years duration now suffers his own flow of blood, which she arrests a moment with her cloth touched to his face. She said: "If I but touch his clothes, I will be made well" (Mk 5:28). And Jesus made her body well, and she became beautiful. She was now no longer unclean. Veronica saw the human face of Jesus, the suffering face of humankind, and to her was given the holy face of Jesus, the divine face of compassion that thirsts for communion with us in this world. "See, the home of God is among mortals. He will dwell with them as their God; they will be his peoples, and God himself will be with them; he will wipe every tear from their eyes. Death will be no more; mourning and crying and pain will be no more, for the first things have passed away" (Rev 21:3-4).

Compassion arises because people love one another, and compassion reflects the love of Christ in the world. His image should be imprinted not only on the cloth but also on our hearts. We should live as human beings made in the image of God, with his love drawn on our face. "The thirst for communion is evoked every time I look at Veronica's veil with the face of Christ on it and the face of all whom I love" (Nouwen). The woman who gives Jesus to drink at the well, the woman who washes his feet with her tears and dries them with her hair, Martha who feeds Jesus and Mary who sits at his feet to listen, and Magdalene who comes to the tomb with spices to anoint his dead body—these are the Veronicas all over the world who show the face of Christ. They offer peace not war, hope not despair, life not death, gratitude not resentment, forgiveness not revenge, mercy and not pain. Veronica is a moment of sanctuary for Jesus, a moment of being at home in a woman's arms where all life begins and where it so often ends.

Note

In the Acts of Pilate, found in the apocryphal Gospel of Nicodemus, a woman appears as a witness at the trial of Jesus before Pilate. "And a woman called Bernice crying out from a distance said: 'I had an issue of blood and I touched the hem of his garment, and the issue of blood, which had lasted twelve years, ceased.' [see Mk 5:25-34] The Jews said: 'We have a law not to permit a woman to give testimony'" (Book VII, 1-5). In a later apocryphal reference in the Death of Pilate there is mention of the face of Jesus imprinted on a sudarium (a cloth napkin or veil), but not in the context of the way of the cross.

Bernike or Beronike (Pherenike) is a Greek word, meaning "bearer of victory." Veronica renders the Greek into Latin. Veronica could also be derived from the Latin words, vera and icon, and then Veronica means "true icon." Obviously the Latin derivation fits the story of Veronica, but the Greek derivation is more reliable philologically.

Veronica is not in evidence in the memoirs of the pilgrims to the Holy Land before the Middle Ages. There is nothing about her in the oldest historical martyrologies. As with many such wonderful legends of the saints, we have no reliable historical evidence that attests to the event. We also have no evidence to the contrary. That a woman along the way of the cross stepped forward in compassion to wipe the face of Jesus is surely possible, however, and even plausible.

Her skin soaked soothing feels so kind.
Tender, tracing, cloth and cool.
A grassy field waters
a plowed face.

A verdant pasture on neck's nape.
Trickling cold and splinter sweat blend.
A risky touch tries so hard
to heal.

Prayer

God of Kindness, you created humankind
    in your very image and likeness.
In this station we contemplate one called "True Image."
    She is the "True image" of the Compassionate God.
She scoured away the pungent filth of the world
    to unmask the face of Him
who is "the reflection of God's glory,
    the exact representation of God's Being."
    This gentle woman is the personification of Sophia,
"the spotless mirror of the power of God,
    the image of his goodness."
May we, in our own lives,
    strive by deeds of loving kindness
    to unveil your divine image
before the faces of all men and women.
                                            Amen.

Intercessions

Response: Women of worth, intercede for us.

That we may remember—in the ecstasy of joy—that we bear the image and likeness of God:
> Women of worth, intercede for us.

That we, like the Pharisee women of Jesus' time, may minister to society's victims:
> Women of worth, intercede for us.

That the Holy Spirit may breathe compassion and discretion into all with authority over transgressors:
> Women of worth, intercede for us.

That we may not turn our faces from those who are physically unsightly, but seek the presence of God within them:
> Women of worth, intercede for us.

That the church and society may acknowledge in practice the role and contribution of women:
> Women of worth, intercede for us.

Jesus Falls the Second Time

VII

Simon is trying to speak to Jesus, and no doubt to encourage him to get up. Jesus is kneeling down, straddling the cross. He has one arm around Simon, whose headdress distinguishes him as a common laborer. The artist has yoked Station Six and Station Seven. It may well be that when Jesus fell there was a moment of delay that allowed Veronica to approach him and console him, before Simon could assist him to rise yet again.

Blessed are the poor in spirit, for theirs is the kingdom of heaven.
———Matthew 5:3

"I am poured out like water, and all my bones are out of joint; my heart is like wax; it is melted within my breast; my mouth is dried up like a potsherd, and my tongue sticks to my jaws; you lay me in the dust of death" (Ps 22:14-15). If the first fall came as a surprise to Jesus, it must have also raised fear in him. A second fall would have brought terror. Perhaps, he realizes, his body will not carry him all the way. How is it then to end? When he first falls, he is dragged and beaten to drive him to get up on his feet and walk forward. The second fall, then, becomes a terrifying glimpse of what is to come. His prostration is a prediction of suffering beyond his control. Jesus must have been drowning in unsurpassable anguish. "From on high he sent fire; it went deep into my bones; he spread a net for my feet; he turned me back; he has left me stunned, faint all day long. My transgressions were bound into a yoke; by his hand they were fastened together; they weigh on my neck, sapping my strength; the Lord handed me over to those whom I cannot withstand" (Lam 1:13-14).

The "slings and arrows of outrageous fortune" leave so many—perhaps most of us—spent, burnt out, finally fallen under the weight of the burdens of the daily lifetime cross. Fatigue, wear and tear, the very genetic chemistry of our blood, bring on our collapse. Henry David Thoreau said of everyday human living: "the mass of men lead lives of quiet desperation." Who are we? What are we? So much within us and so much without us is out of our hands. We watch ourselves fall unable to catch ourselves in time. We lament our ancestors or our times, we blame our enemies without or our failings within, we regret our circumstances or our choices, but fall we do and trapped we are all too often. And so Jesus was flat on the ground, dead tired, and in anguish about what was to come.

Of suffering and evil God gives human beings no explanation to answer our perennial question: why? why me? and why not me? Jesus fallen on the way to Calvary was God's response to our pain. God with us. Emmanuel. God did not give us words of illumination. Our God-in-Jesus-made-flesh gave us his body. Not an argument but a demonstration. In solidarity with our way of the cross Jesus carried his cross that was our cross. I will join you, he said. I will weep with you. I will walk through it all with you. I will fall with you, and not just once, but over again as you do, so that your despair may become mine and my hope become your hope.

Note

The second fall follows three episodes or stations of consolation. His mother Mary encounters Jesus; Simon lifts the cross of Jesus; Veronica wipes the face of Jesus. It is less likely that Jesus continued to fall after Simon was enlisted to assist him, and perhaps even to carry the cross. Of course, we do not know exactly what Simon was doing, nor do we know the physical condition of Jesus. We can readily imagine Jesus was almost dead on his feet. What might be concluded is that the order of the stations of the cross does not pretend to report events in a necessary sequence. Perhaps all of Jesus' falls were prior to Simon's assistance. It does not matter to us to know exactly what happened. The seven stations of the cross that make up the actual walking with the wood of the cross (3-9) intermingle three downfalls (3, 7, 9) and four upholdings (4, 5, 6, 8) by various people of help to Jesus along the way to Calvary. Episodes of desolation when Jesus is down alternate with episodes of consolation when the various women and Simon of Cyrene offer their support.

Now gravity is an enemy too.
Shoulders surge and sink,
the knees can't seem to think
about where they're supposed to be.

Everything stops but pain.
"All the way, all the way," like she told you.
Keep moving, no proving
anything to anyone, now.

Now gravity is a dancing partner.
Foot, flat, I lead, he leads,
Woozy but upright, the body pleads
its silent, waltzing case.

Prayer

Jesus, our brother, you declined the numbing myrrh and wine.
> In this your second fall we see the epitome of our human frailty.
> We succumb to physical weakness, to depression, to boredom, to frustration.
Frequently we strive to counter this with the "high" of drugs, the oblivion
> of alcohol,
>> the release of pent-up inner violence.
> Focus our eyes upon you, lying prostrate,
>> groveling in the dust and flies,
> the scurrilous howl of the crowds pounding your ears.
Teach us, like you, to rise
> through strength of human will
>> and the intoxication of the Spirit's grace.
>>> Amen.

Intercessions

Response: Jesus, numb with grief, vibrant with the Spirit, hear us.

For those who have fallen from God's grace and quenched the Holy Spirit within them:
 Jesus, numb with grief, vibrant with the Spirit, hear us.

For those who succumb to addictions, that they may be inebriated by the Holy Spirit:
 Jesus, numb with grief, vibrant with the Spirit, hear us.

For those who do not understand another's anguish or addiction:
 Jesus, numb with grief, vibrant with the Spirit, hear us.

For those depleted in body and mind, that your life blood may transfuse them, the power of the Spirit seep through their limbs:
 Jesus, numb with grief, vibrant with the Spirit, hear us.

In thanksgiving for the times the Spirit or a human being has raised us up:
 Jesus, numb with grief, vibrant with the Spirit, hear us.

Jesus Speaks With the Daughters of Jerusalem

Jesus has stopped with the cross. He stands with one arm around the upright beam and the weight off his shoulders. Simon remains in the far background, hardly visible except for his one hand above the wood that steadies the crossbeam. Three women and an older child are looking out the window of a house that borders the street. The women look not at Jesus but at us. They seem resigned. Their washed clothes have been put out to dry on the window sill. A small naked child is alone and outside, casting a shadow in front of him as he toddles toward Jesus. Perhaps that darkness foreshadows the future, for when this child has grown to maturity, the whole city of Jerusalem will be brutalized and razed by the Roman armies.

Blessed are those who mourn, for they will be comforted.
——Matthew 5:4

Who cares for the caretaker? Some women of Jerusalem weep in sorrow for Jesus as he passes by. Jesus often wept for others in sorrow. Jesus loved Mary and Martha, and when Lazarus died and both of his sisters were mourning him, Jesus wept for them all and raised Lazarus from the tomb (Jn 11). When Jesus looked over the city of Jerusalem, whose daughters and sons he so loved, he wept over the city, which was rejecting the one who truly cared for her. "'If you, even you, had only recognized on this day the things that make for peace! But now they are hidden from your eyes. Indeed, the days will come upon you, when your enemies will set up ramparts around you and surround you, and hem you in on every side. They will crush you to the ground, you and your children within you, and they will not leave within you one stone upon another; because you did not recognize the time of your visitation from God" (Lk 19:42-44). In the not-too-distant future Jerusalem would be abused by the foreign empire that loved her not. "When you see Jerusalem surrounded by armies, then know that its desolation has come near. . . . For there will be great distress on the earth and wrath against this people; they will fall by the edge of the sword and be taken away as captives among all nations; and Jerusalem will be trampled on by the Gentiles, until the times of the Gentiles are fulfilled" (Lk 21:20-24).

Now in the last hours of his own life the compassion of Jesus continues to flow for the daughters of Jerusalem who mourn for him: "Daughters of Jerusalem, do not weep for me, but weep for yourselves and for your children. For the days are surely coming when they will say, 'Blessed are the barren, and the wombs that never bore, and the breasts that never nursed.' Then they will begin to say to the mountains, 'Fall on us'; and to the hills, 'Cover us.'" (Lk 23:28-30). What a contrast with the woman who raised her voice in an outburst of joy about the mother of Jesus: "Blessed is the womb that bore you and the breasts that nursed you!" (Lk 11:27). In this momentary pause on the way to Calvary, life-givers weep over death-dealers. The women weep over Jesus crushed by Rome that was the hostile instrument of his own people. Jesus weeps over the daughters of Jerusalem who would be crushed by Rome that was the future enemy of his own people. "Jerusalem, Jerusalem, the city that kills the prophets and stones those who are sent to it! How often have I desired to gather your children together as a hen gathers her brood under her wings, and you were not willing! See, your house is left to you, desolate" (Mt 23:37-38). Life so worth living is so often snuffed out. Violence without compassion dominates the story of humanity. It is "Rachel weeping for her children . . . because they are no more" (Mt 2:18). It is the Lord Jesus with a woman's compassion weeping for God's children who are no more. "My eyes flow with rivers of tears because of the destruction of my people. . . . My eyes cause me grief at the fate of all the young women in my city" (Lam 3:48-51). That the good die young reveals the human condition shared with us by the Son of God. And, such agony is a "sorrow too deep for tears."

If the crucifixion is what is done to Jesus without provocation of the Romans, what will it be like when the Romans are truly provoked with the people of Jerusalem? "For if they do this when the wood is green, what will happen when it is dry?" Jerusalem itself was to be crucified. "'Here is your King!' . . . 'We have no king but the emperor'" (Jn 19:14-15) will seem an ironic commentary upon a dark future.

Jesus ministers to the women and children of Jerusalem while walking the way of the cross. Even amid suffering Jesus is saving those he encounters. The good thief crucified beside Jesus comes to salvation at the last moment of his life. To the very end of his days Jesus is saving us, and ever after we know that suffering can be saving and that pain can be redemptive.

Note

The women of Jerusalem who speak to Jesus along the way of the cross are recorded only in Luke (23:27-31). The evangelist Luke in all probability wrote after the Roman army had razed Jerusalem and scattered its inhabitants in the year 70 AD because of their chronic rebellion against the Roman empire. We are not sure who these women were. It is possible that the women along the way are the same women who follow Jesus to the end. A group of women are reported on Calvary at a distance from the cross in all the synoptic gospels. Mary Magdalene, Mary the mother of James and Joseph (probably the same person referred to also as "the wife of Clopas" and as "his mother's sister"), and the mother of the sons of Zebedee (James and John, and she is named Salome in Mark) are mentioned. Three women, "his mother, and his mother's sister, Mary the wife of Clopas, and Mary Magdalene" are named in John (19:25). Consequently, depictions of the eighth station of the cross often have three women, usually with babies in their arms in harmony with the words of Jesus to the women of Jerusalem in Luke's gospel to weep for themselves and for their children.

Other than the beloved disciple (Jn 19:26-27) none of the disciples are present on the way of the cross or on Calvary hill. The men were afraid. What was happening to Jesus might happen to them. The women may have been more caring or more courageous than the men. The women may also have been less threatened than the men, since women might not have been taken as seriously as potential conspirators. We do not know what risks of arrest these women were taking, but surely they opened themselves to abuse and ridicule.

101

Are the clothes drying?
Which child is crying?

And who is this thing
the bastards are killing today?
A little bone of a man,
he'll barely make it up the hill.

Are the clothes drying?
Which child is crying?

This man bleeds brutally.
His shocky skin can barely sweat.
What threat
did he pose?

Are the clothes drying?
Which child is crying?

She says it is that Nazarene.
Well those people are lost for sure.
And after that scene in the Temple,
if the soldiers don't kill him
the lenders will.

Are the clothes drying?
Which child is crying?

My, what dust they raise
when they blaze down the road
their horses and spears and whips.
The curious and the cruel
just shoving this fool
up the hill he'll never walk down.

Are the clothes drying?
Which child is crying?

Prayer

Jesus, you are led as king and convict.
    The shrill wail, the plangent dirge,
the celebratory poems and the limping rhythm
    of the professional women mourners
is like balm to your soul.[3]
    The regal lamentation "Alas! Lord, alas! Majesty!"
echoes the devotion of the multitude joyous on Palm Sunday.
    From this crowd of sympathizers you selected the wise women.
    To them you spoke as a prophet-martyr.
    You predicted a dual death wail,
over yourself and over Jerusalem.
    Before her walls the Romans would crucify five hundred persons a day,[4]
    multiplying your atrocious fate by thousands.
    We are mindful that our hands hold the possibility
of utterly obliterating your wondrous world.
    Let our ears be open to your warnings
and our hearts and minds zealous, not to destroy, but to re-create.
                       Amen.

Intercessions

Response: Women of compassion, intercede for us.

For those who mourn, especially over the violent death of their loved ones:
   Women of compassion, intercede for us.

For those who conduct funerals and those who counsel mourners, that they may understand the mystery of the resurrection:
   Women of compassion, intercede for us.

For the simplification of the process of dying and of funeral rites:
   Women of compassion, intercede for us.

For an awareness of the tragedy of mass death:
   Women of compassion, intercede for us.

For a balance between grief and hope:
   Women of compassion, intercede for us.

Jesus Falls the Third Time

IX

Jesus is flat on his back, and the cross is pressed into the ground by the force of his fall. He is in position to be nailed down. Dead tired, he is dead on his back. His arms are wide spread and his legs open. Exhausted and vulnerable, Jesus is spent. There is no Simon in sight and no help at hand.

Blessed are the meek, for they will inherit the earth.
——Matthew 5:5

"All we like sheep have gone astray; we have all turned to our own way, and the Lord has laid on him the iniquity of us all. He was oppressed, and he was afflicted, yet he did not open his mouth; like a lamb that is led to the slaughter, and like a sheep that before its shearers is silent, so he did not open his mouth" (Is 53:6-7). Jesus is no longer falling. Jesus is fallen. Three falls and he is defeated. He is a beaten man. If the first fall generated fear and the second fall terror, the third fall brings desperation. One fall may be an accident, two remains a question, but three becomes a pattern. The future is seen in this falling that carries a prediction. Jesus is trapped in a body of weakness that he knows he cannot escape. "Surely everyone stands as a mere breath. Surely everyone goes about like a shadow" (Ps 39:5-6).

Our body is but a thin envelope cupping warm water, a speck of conscious stardust on the surface of a burnt-out cinder in a vast universe. We are but earth. As the liturgy of Ash Wednesday says: "Remember you are dust and to dust you shall return." Covered with sweat and blood, Jesus fallen to the ground must have seemed a vessel of weakness. "But we have this treasure in clay jars" (2 Cor 4:7). Here was a wrestler fallen in the earth of the combatant ring, only to become covered all over with the potter's clay. Here is Jacob wrestling with the angel, who knocks his legs out from under him. Jesus falls to God before whom no mortal flesh can stand. In the surrender of the clay of his body Jesus wrestles with God as must we all do. His hope, like ours, is not to win but to lose, "for whenever I am weak, then I am strong" (2 Cor 12:10).

Someone helped Jesus to his feet. Perhaps unfriendly or indifferent soldiers pulled him up. Jesus needed another to carry the burden of salvation with him and for him. In the three falls of Jesus along the way to Calvary we embrace our own falls, for no flesh may stand on its own. And yet we ever hope in the saving ways of God. "For God's foolishness is wiser than human wisdom, and God's weakness is stronger than human strength" (1 Cor 1:25).

The leaves are falling, falling as if from far away,
like fading gardens deep in the sky;
they fall with gestures of denial.

And through the night the heavy earth falls,
through the stars into aloneness.

All of us fall. This hand does fall.
Look upon all the others—everyone, everywhere.

And yet there is one who holds all this falling ever gently in his hands.

—"Autumn" by Rainer Maria Rilke, trans. Nicholas Ayo

Note

The three falls carry a special symbolism. In the Bible, whatever happens three times is shorthand for an event that truly happened. Three times Elijah soaks the wood of the holocaust with water and we know it is really wet, so that when he calls down fire from heaven there can be no question of its vigor. Three times the devil tempts Jesus in the desert and three times he does not consent, and we know that Jesus did not sin. Jesus goes off alone in the Garden of Gethsemane three times, and three times his disciples fall asleep. We know he indeed prayed in fear and trembling, even sweating blood in Luke's account, and that the disciples certainly were asleep to what was happening to Jesus and to what would happen to them. They would enter into temptation. Put to the test, they would fail him. Peter denies Jesus three times in the courtyard of the high priest, and we know he surely failed his master. Three times Jesus falls under the weight of the cross, and we know without doubt that Jesus fell, crushed by his burden. Three times a nail is driven into his flesh, and we know he was truly wed to the wood, truly crucified hands and feet in agony. The empty tomb will be discovered on the third day, and we know that Jesus was without doubt dead and then rose from the grave. Three times after the resurrection Jesus will ask Peter if he loves him, and three times Peter will answer "you know that I love you" (Jn 21:15-18). And we know that Peter is graciously forgiven by the risen Lord.

Nothing remains
but
to sink.

Trying
not to think

that the kindest thing
you'll drink

is
wood.

Prayer

Jesus, God of dying and rising,
   you said that unless a grain of wheat
fall in the ground and die, it cannot rise.
   In your third fall we see
   the God "who shares in the absurdities and horrors of our world,"[5] even our
godforsakenness.
   Yet, through your joyful hope in the resurrection,
you ran your race and became the pioneer and perfector of our faith.[6]
   By your Spirit enable us
         to turn brutal force into vital energy
               and to lead humanity back to the poetry of life.
                     Amen.

Intercessions

Response: God of dying and rising, hear us.

For the victims of genocide, massacre, and mass starvation:
God of dying and rising, hear us.

For those who are convinced of the absence of God:
God of dying and rising, hear us.

For those who feel forsaken by God:
God of dying and rising, hear us.

For those who have no hope in the resurrection:
God of dying and rising, hear us.

For the gentling of the world:
God of dying and rising, hear us.

Jesus Is Stripped of His Garments

One of the garments of Jesus is thrown to the ground. Another garment is coming off. The soldier walks away, applying force to the pulling, with no regard or respect shown toward Jesus. Jesus stands in mute pain. Standing by him is another soldier or perhaps an underling. The artist has combined the third fall and the arrival at Calvary, where the stripping of the prisoner would have been the first order of business. The implication is that Jesus fell right before he came to the end of the road and that he was completely spent, stripped already of his strength, and soon stripped down to his bare body.

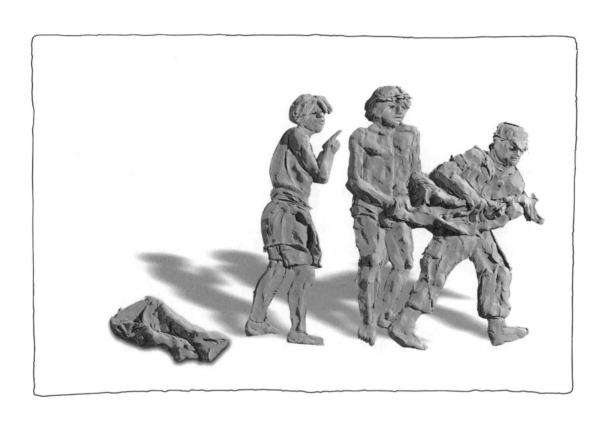

> Blessed are the meek, for they will inherit the earth.
> ——Matthew 5:5

"O my people, what have I done to you? In what have I wearied you? Answer me!" (Mi 6:3) To appreciate the horror of the crucifixion one need not imagine that the soldiers were particularly cruel, though they might have been. No doubt frequent crucifixions made soldiers assigned to execution a callous group. Perhaps there was no other way for them to survive their duty. Or perhaps they had a sadistic streak that recommended them. We do not know. We do know that any cruelty was permitted, and those condemned to die by crucifixion were spared no torment their executioners might be bothered to inflict. Dante's dire warning to "abandon all hope ye who enter here" fits crucifixion just as well as entry into hell. Stripping the victim of his clothes was standard procedure. "When the soldiers had crucified Jesus, they took his clothes and divided them into four parts, one for each soldier. They also took his tunic; now the tunic was seamless, woven in one piece from the top. So they said to one another, 'Let us not tear it, but cast lots for it to see who will get it'" (Jn 19:23-24). To the victor went the spoils, and the clothing of the victim was probably a round form of compensation for their labors. "They divided my clothes among themselves, and for my clothing they cast lots" (Jn 19:24 quoting Ps 22:18).

118

The crucified was intended to be a spectacle of pain and humiliation. The victim writhing in pain was reduced as much as possible to a thing, killed in front of everyone. Such a horrific death fed a bloodlust in some spectators and a sober fear of falling afoul of the law in others. One can assume these soldiers were all business. They would want to finish their work before the sabbath sundown, for the Romans were willing to recognize local customs in the hope of social harmony. If the garments were stuck to Jesus' wounds by the dried blood, that was not their problem. His own clothes were pulled off like bandages by hands accustomed to crucifixion unto death. They were careful not to tear the cloth of his tunic, but Jesus in his flesh was torn and stood a spectacle for humiliation and mockery. Bruised and bloodied, Jesus must have stood alone naked and half-dead in the sight of a surrounding and mostly pitiless crowd. He was a worm and no man, "So marred was his appearance, beyond human semblance, and his form beyond that of mortals" (Is 52:14). From his nipples to his groin he was a target for pain and ridicule. There was no cover for him in this terrible moment.

Jesus had been embarrassed when they dragged out the woman taken in adultery, "making her stand before all of them" (Jn 8:3). The onlooking circle of men was ready to stone her to death. Jesus knelt down with eyes lowered and scribbled on the ground with his finger. When others undress us against our will for their own pitiless gaze, we are never more an object. The body is not unwrapped as a personal gift, but exposed as a mere thing. The Lord of love was not admired on Calvary hill. His body was exposed and betrayed to those who would cast unfeeling eyes upon it. It was worth nothing, covered with nothing but three iron nails and a veil of blood.

"Naked I came from my mother's womb, and naked shall I return there; the Lord gave, and the Lord has taken away" (Job 1:21). However we die, we are all poor and dependent, and our flesh is naked. We will all be stripped in death even of that thin skin that is our first and last garment. We are our body, and our body is ever vulnerable, as was the body of Jesus before he was to be crucified on the hill of Calvary.

Note

In Roman practice the criminal was led to the place of crucifixion naked, carrying the crossbeam on his shoulders, and being beaten en route. In deference to the Jewish abhorrence of public nudity, Jesus was led along the way of the cross dressed in his own clothes. On Calvary he was stripped, and probably naked to public view. It is possible that in deference to Jewish sensibilities the crucified criminals in Jerusalem were given a loincloth, as is claimed in the Acts of Pilate. That his clothes were taken from him and distributed among the soldiers, however, suggests he was left with little or nothing.

John mentions five pieces of clothing (probably sandals, belt, head covering, outer mantle or cloak, and the inner tunic). It is that inner tunic, a long garment that lay closest to the skin, that the soldiers were unwilling to divide into pieces. The gospels say it was a seamless garment, woven of one piece of cloth. Probably it was a garment of the poor, a rectangular weaving with an opening for the head and the front and back sides fastened together in some fashion to make a tubular piece of underclothing.

1

The newspaper
covering a roadside's dead deer
sails off in a truck's dirty
wind wake.

2

The cloth clinging
to his soldier-beaten skin
gives in to an officer's
rushed disgust.

A garment grinding
amid earth and soldier
squeezed and pulled
from crotch and shoulder,

pressed twixt hammer and stone
beating sticks stammer and groan:

a naked man
is always a dying man.

Prayer

Jesus, full of empathy for the vulnerable,
   we contemplate your exposure by the brazen soldiers.
Clothes are part of our personality,
   an element of our dignity.
You are stripped, you are naked,
   you are exposed to the coarseness and quips of the crowd.
In your humiliation,
   come in your tangible presence
to all those subjected to a similar mortification.
   Cover their nakedness with your glory,
convert the gross handling they receive
   into the tender caresses of your healing hands,
restore their dignity as
   exquisite images of the divine.
                              Amen.

Intercessions

Response: Jesus, divested but clothed in glory, hear us.

For an obliteration of pornography:
    Jesus, divested but clothed in glory, hear us.

For a realization of the dignity of the human body:
    Jesus, divested but clothed in glory, hear us.

For those who design clothing, that they may strive to illuminate the beauty of the corporal temples of the Holy Spirit:
    Jesus, divested but clothed in glory, hear us.

For those who pursue fashion that they may shun provocative garb and honor instead the dignity and elegance of the human body:
    Jesus, divested but clothed in glory, hear us.

For those who depict the body in art and film, that they may be inspired by the purity of the Holy Spirit:
    Jesus, divested but clothed in glory, hear us.

Jesus Is Nailed to the Cross

Jesus is supine. There are four nails for his hands and his feet. He gives his left hand to the soldier, who does not hold his arm but only the nail and the hammer. The good thief, called Dismas in legend, is crucified on a T-shaped cross to the left of Jesus. The artist suggests another means of crucifixion: rather than being nailed, this thief's arms and feet are tied to the cross. Tradition has shown Jesus nailed to a cross with an upright beam that reaches above the crossbeam. Over his head they would nail a sign saying: "Jesus of Nazareth, King of the Jews" (I. N. R. I., which means in Latin, Jesus Nazarenus, Rex Judaeorum).

Blessed are the peacemakers, for they will be called children of God.

————Matthew 5:9

"And with him they crucified two bandits, one on his right and one on his left" (Mk 15:27). Jesus is lifted on a cross as a spectacle under the sun of high noon before a multitude come to watch a man in agony die by inches. They nailed him fast to his cross. "My hands and feet have shriveled; I can count all my bones. They stare and gloat over me" (Ps 22:16-17).

Jesus laid hands of healing upon so many people—the sick, the paralyzed, the deaf, the blind, and those possessed of evil spirits. There is nothing more human than the human touch. Helping hands, loving hands, a woodsmith's sturdy hands, those gentle hands of Jesus that touched our raw wounds. The hands of God were laid on our pain, and the hand of Jesus blessed us in our dying. How could we nail those living hands to a dead tree? Soft intricate flesh that can craft beauty and caress the body, that can speak in tongues and heal injuries, masterpiece of ensouled body united to divinity, how could it be so trashed?

When the prodigal son comes back home, the prodigal father insists that they put a ring on his finger and shoes on his feet (Lk 15:22). Only the children of the household wore shoes. Jesus was offended when Simon the Pharisee invited him to table but did not tell his servants to bathe his weary feet as was the customary hospitality. The unnamed woman in the gospel of Luke washes the feet of Jesus with her tears and dries them with her long hair (Lk 7:36-50). And much to their embarrassment, Jesus washes the feet of his own disciples. "So if I, your Lord and Teacher, have washed your feet, you also ought to wash one another's feet" (Jn 13:14). Now, the soldiers who stand for our human violence nail the feet of this Jesus to the wood of a tree cut down in its prime.

> *This thong, I know, will last;*
> *Draw out the arm and make it fast;*
> *Through hand and board with strength*
> *Drive the nail of mickle length.*
> *Now, King of the Jews, in the sun*
> *Gape, for our work is done.*
>
> —*Author unknown*

Even in the womb, the unborn child has ridges on its fingers that are its own prints. We identify our body by scars that cannot be changed. Our unique wounds contain our own history and no one else's. We are our body. Jesus appeared to his disciples on Easter Sunday evening and said: "Why are you frightened, and why do doubts arise in your hearts? Look at my hands and my feet; see that it is I myself.

Touch me and see; for a ghost does not have flesh and bones as you see that I have" (Lk 24:38-39). Hands and feet were nailed to the cross, but the wounds of Jesus became glorious forever. This world is not discarded in eternity, nor our humanity undone by death. All the way of the cross is transfigured unto glory. The body of Jesus remains a witness to the fidelity of God that would not abandon us, even when we took the life of those hands and those feet so cruelly nailed to that wood on that day long ago. "He himself bore our sins in his body on the cross, so that, free from sins, we might live for righteousness; by his wounds you have been healed" (1 Pt 2:24).

Note

Crucifixions were carried out in several ways. Some victims of crucifixion were tied to the cross and left to hang on the cross beam. Others were tied to an upright stake and left in that position to die. Still others were nailed to the cross. What the custom in Jerusalem may have been is not known for sure. In archeological excavations, only one skeleton from that period has been found with indications of crucifixion by nailing. The biblical evidence stems from the words of Thomas, who in his doubt proclaimed he would not believe unless he put his finger in the wounds of Jesus made by the nails: "Unless I see the mark of the nails in his hands, and put my finger in the mark of the nails and my hand in his side, I will not believe" (Jn 20:25; see also Luke 24:38-39).

If Jesus was nailed to the cross, it would have been more easily done while he was lying on the ground. His hands would have been nailed through the wrist rather than the palms, so that the wrist bones might support his weight. The crossbeam with the victim attached would then be lifted to the vertical post, which was probably already in position. Then the feet would be tied or nailed. Probably the nails were driven into each ankle rather than the arch of the foot. Perhaps the feet straddled the vertical beam, so that the nails might be driven sideways. With the weight of the body unsupported, breathing would be very difficult, and death would come sooner. Sometimes there was a footrest or a small platform where the crucified could lean the weight of his body. Such devices were not a mercy but a way of prolonging the death agony. Because Jesus died so soon, we may infer that nothing special was done to prolong his dying. Whatever happened to Jesus in his crucifixion, we can be sure it was atrocious in its pain and that the brutality was intended as the substance of this horrible way of death.

Hold the nail
and pound.

Hold the nail
and pound.

Fingers claw and stretch
for air they cannot catch.

Faces wince and turn
from sounds they did not learn
about in Isaiah.

Hold the nail
and pound.

Hold the nail
and pound.

Toes splay toward paths unwalked.
Feet bend like a hurt dog's head cocked
to one side asking why.

Hold the nail
and pound.

Hold the nail
and pound.

Soldiers perfect these two moves
like the centuries' slow turn.
Are we done? Are there more?
The lesson taught
is the lesson learned:
Executed skin can be
split or burned.

Hold the nail
and pound.

Hold the nail
and pound.

Prayer

Boundless Creator, God of power and victory,
    we are confronted with the terror of human freedom.
Your skillful hands painted the multicolored world
    and fashioned the intricate elegance of humankind.
    At your feet all should bow.
Yet, humankind chose to transfix those hands to a crossbar,
    to pinion those feet to a gibbet.
But in your weakness is your strength,
    in your fetters lies your freedom.
From this mangled carcass
    life and liberty will burgeon, unrestrained.
Teach us to treasure true freedom,
    to monitor our wills with discretion,
        to feel your limitless Spirit
            in every straightened circumstance,
          to transform pain into glory.
            Amen.

Intercessions

Response: God, bound, yet boundless, hear us.

For the grace to look beyond the physical sufferings of Christ into the anguish of the Godhead:
>God, bound, yet boundless, hear us.

For a transformation of pain into glory:
>God, bound yet boundless, hear us.

For those who, like Jesus, cry, "My God, my God, why have you forsaken me?":
>God, bound yet boundless, hear us.

For a vision of the life-bearing hope embedded in suffering:
>God, bound yet boundless, hear us.

In thanksgiving for those who have inspired us by their courage in suffering:
>God, bound yet boundless, hear us.

Jesus Is Crucified and Dies

XII

The centurion with a machine gun stands in the background to the right side of Jesus. Mary and John stand to the left near the foot of the cross. Jesus is looking straight ahead at us. The positioning of the hands and feet is asymmetrical. One hand is raised higher and nailed through the wrist. The other hand is nailed through the palm. His right foot is nailed to the front of the vertical beam and the left foot to one side. Jesus is covered with a loin cloth. The crucifixion is not tidy; there is no presentable Jesus. His figure is depicted between the abandonment of the cross and the triumph of the cross. The artist thereby suggests both the present desolation and the future exaltation of Jesus.

> Blessed are those who are persecuted for righteousness' sake,
> for theirs is the kingdom of heaven.
> ——Matthew 5:10

We can be brief. Jesus was hung upright to die. Having been nailed to the cross while lying, Jesus would have then been lifted up. Three hours were long enough to drain away his life; three minutes were long enough to seem forever. The victim was left to die under the sun before whomever wished to watch the agonizing time pass. "I am poured out like water, and all my bones are out of joint; my heart is like wax; it is melted within my breast; my mouth is dried up like a potsherd, and my tongue sticks to my jaws; you lay me in the dust of death. For dogs are all around me; a company of evildoers encircles me" (Ps 22:14-16).

The gospels tell of those who mocked Jesus. His enemies quoted his words back to him. "You who would destroy the temple and build it in three days, save yourself! If you are the Son of God, come down from the cross" (Mt 27:40). After all "he saved others; he cannot save himself. He is the King of Israel; let him come down from the cross now, and we will believe in him. He trusts in God; let God deliver him now, if he wants to; for he said, 'I am God's Son'" (Mt 27:42-43). Just as in the separation of the sheep and the goats in the judgment account (Mt 25:31-46), two thieves were crucified with him, one on his right and one on his left. One thief is resentful and despairing and chooses death, while the other is grateful and hopeful and chooses life. "Truly I tell you, today you will be with me in Paradise" (Lk 23:43). "And I, when I am lifted up from the earth, will draw all people to myself" (Jn 12:32). The Roman soldiers offered him to drink of sour wine, probably given in derision and without pity. At the foot of the cross only a sole centurion gave true witness: "Truly this man was God's Son!" (Mk 15:39).

To Mary, the angel Gabriel brought tidings of great joy. Her Lord God would be dependent upon his mother for his life in this world, as she was dependent upon her Creator for her own. Now she is present as Jesus becomes mother, giving birth to the church in his dying on Calvary hill. "When Jesus saw his mother and the disciple whom he loved standing beside her, he said to his mother, 'Woman, here is your son.' Then he said to the disciple, 'Here is your mother'" (Jn 19:26-27). Mother Mary, Mother Jesus, Mother Church.

God the Father shaped the lovely Eve, mother of the living, from a rib in Adam's side while he slept. We sinners pierced the heart of God on the cross "and at once blood and water came out" (Jn 19:34). Jesus' own blood, given as our life in the eucharist, together with the waters of baptism flowed out in this birth of the church. His mother Mary nursed him long ago at her breast, but now from his pierced breast Jesus feeds all humankind with an outflow of divine grace. His heart was broken for love of us, and his heart gave its last measure of love in the flood of water and of blood.

"To give all for love is a most sweet bargain" (Julian of Norwich). Jesus died all our deaths, embracing all the sorrows of the world from end to end with arms outstretched. "When they look on the one whom they have pierced, they shall mourn for him, as one mourns for an only child, and weep bitterly over him, as one weeps over a firstborn" (Zec 12:10). The old tree of life in the middle of the garden of Paradise has been supplanted as axis of the world by this new tree of life fruitful on Calvary hill. "Behold the wood of the cross on which hung the Savior of the world." When Jesus gave his life, "at that moment the curtain of the temple was torn in two, from top to bottom. The earth shook, and the rocks were split. The tombs also were opened, and many bodies of the saints who had fallen asleep were raised" (Mt 27:51-52). Here is the rebirthing of the whole creation, now become new born children of God's love given to the last, and once and for all. Indeed, "love is strong as death, passion fierce as the grave. Its flashes are flashes of fire, a raging flame" (Sg 8:6).

Note

In Mark's gospel Jesus is crucified at about nine o'clock in the morning, and he dies at about three o'clock in the afternoon. In Matthew's gospel we read: "From noon on, darkness came over the whole land until three in the afternoon" (27:45). Mark may be giving the liturgical prayer hours of a Good Friday liturgy transposed into the gospel account itself. Tradition has held that it took but three hours for Jesus to die, and when Pilate was asked to deliver the body for burial, he was surprised to learn that Jesus was dead so soon (Mk 15:44-45).

Jesus was severely flogged as an exemplary punishment before he was condemned to crucifixion, and he must have been weakened. Loss of blood and wounds caused by beatings or falls along the way to Calvary made matters all the worse. Hence his exhaustion in carrying the cross and his needing assistance from Simon of Cyrene. The cause of death from crucifixion is some combination of dehydration, loss of blood, and in particular, shock. All these conditions are exacerbated by the difficulty to raise the chest to breathe normally while hanging from a vertical cross.

Golgotha, which is Hebrew for "The Place of the Skull" (Jn 19:17), or Calvary, which is the Latin term taken from the Greek, was the site of crucifixion. It was probably part of a rock quarry not far off the main road and near the wall of the city of Jerusalem. The hill of Calvary was probably a slight outcropping of a harder rock that had been isolated from the easier stone cutting around it. In shape it somewhat resembled a human skull, and hence the popular name arose. Constantine built on the location a basilica, which was burned by the Persians in the seventh century. The church was rebuilt and then burned again by the Moslems in the tenth century. The Crusader church of 1149 (with modifications) remains standing to this day.

The four gospels record seven last words of Jesus. These seven "sentences" are important as the last words of a dying man, and they vary in content and emotion much as the various gospel portraits of Jesus differ one from the other. Mark and Matthew record the cry of the cross: "My God, my God, why have you forsaken me?" (taken from Ps 22:1 and recorded in the Aramaic mother tongue of Jesus). In Luke's gospel Jesus says, "Father, forgive them, for they do not know what they are doing," and he promises the good thief, "today you will be with me in Paradise." Jesus' last word in Luke is a peaceful one: "Father, into your hands I commend my spirit" (taken from Ps 31:5). John's gospel shows a more triumphant Jesus. When Jesus says "I am thirsty," it would seem to be for love more than for water, and in his last moments, Jesus calmly gives the beloved disciple to his mother, "Woman, here is your son," and the mother to the disciple, "Here is your mother." Then with the sovereignty of one whose life is not taken but given, Jesus calmly declares, "It is finished," and only then does he give up his spirit.

As far as we know, Jesus wrote nothing in his lifetime. Little was written about him while he was alive. Here, however, Pilate had written an inscription in Hebrew, Latin, and Greek. Nailed to the cross and "over his head they put the charge against him" (Mt 27:37). "Jesus of Nazareth, the King of the Jews" (Jn 19:19). In Latin, the words are *Jesus Nazarenus, Rex Judaeorum*, abbreviated I.N.R.I.

What is the sound of a dead man breathing?
When corpses are guarded by soldiers' seething?

What is the sound of his mother's gasp?
When held in a mourner's courage clasp?

What do you hear when you listen for breath?
When teeth are stone still and eyes locked by death?

Prayer

Immortal God,
We contemplate the most profound experience of your selfless love,
    the acceptance of death,
the last and most formidable enemy of humankind.
Yet "through the hollow eyes of death,
        I see life peeping."[7]
    On the hideous deathbed you extend to us
        the "right hand of fellowship,"
            the richest element of hope,
                incomparable intimacy with you.
Through this your demise teach us
    that death is but the crucible where all the Spirit's gifts are finally refined,
    that it is the womb that, with the ecstasy of love,
births the newborn into the light of endless day.
                    Amen.

Intercessions

Response: Immortal, vulnerable God, hear our prayer.

That through the grace of the vivifying Spirit we may overcome the fear of death:
   Immortal, vulnerable God, hear our prayer.

That we may see the last breath of the dying as the insufflation of Spirit at Pentecost:
   Immortal, vulnerable God, hear our prayer.

For those who care for the dying, that they may imbibe the breath of the Spirit of those around the cross of Jesus:
   Immortal, vulnerable God, hear our prayer.

For those who suffer from the memories of horrendous deaths in war:
   Immortal, vulnerable God, hear our prayer.

For those who die alone that the Spirit may be palpably present to them:
   Immortal, vulnerable God, hear our prayer.

The Body of Jesus Is Taken Down From the Cross

XIII

Mary is kneeling over the dead body of Jesus stretched out before her on the ground. Her hand veils her face. The woman beside her is consoling her. Joseph of Arimathea is bent over Mary and Jesus, and he holds a young child by the hand. The scene is reminiscent of the Holy Family, and indeed the cross provides a looming background to all human family life, where death is always in view. The inscription nailed to the cross remains nailed to the wood. Pilate insisted: "What I have written, I have written."

> Blessed are those who mourn, for they will be comforted.
> ——Matthew 5:4

Though Jesus was dead, it must have been painful to withdraw the nails from his body and to take him down from the cross in such a broken and shameful position. John's gospel tells of the deposition of the body of Jesus in the hands of Joseph of Arimathea and Nicodemus, two of his hesitant would-be disciples. "Bringing a mixture of myrrh and aloes, weighing about a hundred pounds, they took the body of Jesus and wrapped it with the spices in linen cloths, according to the burial custom of the Jews" (Jn 19:39-40).

The tradition has been that the dead body of Jesus was first laid in his mother's lap and that it received her embrace as its first preparation for burial. The sorrowful mother (the pieta) has been rendered in sculpture and painting through the centuries. The Christian mystery is dramatically presented with the Madonna holding her dead son on her lap. In the ending as in the beginning, his mother Mary holds the body of Jesus to her breast. "Here am I, the servant of the Lord; let it be with me according to your word" (Lk 1:38). The mystery of the incarnation brought to consummation in the paschal mystery of Jesus is simply and poignantly imaged in the figure of Mary and Jesus, yoked together in death as in life.

When gentle hands pulled the nails from the body of Jesus on the cross, those hands were the first kind touch since the Garden of Gethsemane where the Passion of the Lord began. When Jesus was born, a woman washed his body, anointed it with perfume, swaddled his flesh in linen strips of cloth, and laid him in a manger. When Jesus was born into eternal life, a woman washed his body, anointed it with myrrh and aloes, wrapped him in a clean linen cloth shroud, and laid him in the rock. From birth to death, from cradle to the grave, from the womb to the tomb, from Bethlehem to Jerusalem, from Christmas to Easter, from the beginning to the ending, only Mary his mother knew Jesus all the days of his life on this earth. She was conformed to Jesus whom she held in her arms until they belonged to him as well as to her. Mary with her son in her arms takes the whole world to her heart. Human love at its best here embraces divine love at its best. God is carried in the arms of a woman. Holy Mary, mother of God, pray for us sinners, now and at the hour of our death. Amen.

Note

All the evangelists agree that it was Joseph of Arimathea who went to Pilate to secure the body of Jesus immediately after his death and in the early evening.

Of Joseph of Arimathea we know very little. We know Arimathea is a Jewish village, and it is probably the contemporary Rathamin about ten miles northeast of Jerusalem. Mark says that Joseph was "a respected member of the council [the Sanhedrin], who was also himself waiting expectantly for the kingdom of God" (15:43). Matthew says that he was a "rich man," who "went to Pilate and asked for the body of Jesus" (27:57-58). Luke speaks of "a good and righteous man named Joseph, who, though a member of the council, had not agreed to their plan and action" (23:50-51). And John claims he was "a disciple of Jesus, though a secret one because of his fear of the Jews" (19:38).

When the evidence is sifted it may well be that Joseph of Arimathea was a devout Jew who kept the Jewish law that charged him to bury the dead. Like Job or like Tobias he was in all things a righteous man who cared for the dead as Jewish piety required. That he was rich, innocent at the trial of Jesus, and a secret disciple may be later elaborations deemed helpful by the evangelists.

Nicodemus is found only in John's gospel. He was a Pharisee who came to Jesus by night and entered into a long theological conversation with him, in which he would appear to be a sympathizer if not a secret disciple of Jesus (Jn 3:1-17). Later, when the temple police try to arrest Jesus, it is Nicodemus who defends him: "Our law does not judge people without first giving them a hearing to find out what they are doing, does it?" (Jn 7:51)

Her hands
covered her face
the whole time.
She did not look.

His skin
no longer covering bones
much of the time.
He did not look
like much.

A stiffness
like hacked branches
falling off a tree

only to rot
and break away
into nothing

that we can see.

Prayer

God, our Creator and agent of our resurrection,
    you have marvelously fashioned the human body
and made it the temple of your Spirit.
    Grant that, at all times and in all conditions,
we may reverence and cherish this temple,
        even as Nicodemus and Joseph of Arimathea
            cared for the body of the Crucified.
    Give us to understand that humans
            see the outward appearance
                but the Spirit looks into the heart.[8]
                    Amen.

Intercessions

Response: Creator and Re-creator God, hear us.

For those whose loved ones have been denied a decent burial:
Creator and Re-creator God, hear us.

For those who handle the dead, that they may treat reverently the bodies in their care and give glory to God for their skill:
Creator and Re-creator God, hear us.

For care and respect of the bodies of the animal kingdom and a recognition in them also of the ingenuity of the Creator:
Creator and Re-creator God, hear us.

For the bereaved, especially when they view the still, and sometimes maimed, corpses of their loved ones:
Creator and Re-creator God, hear us.

For joy and enthusiasm over the abilities of our own bodies:
Creator and Re-creator God, hear us.

The Body of Jesus
Is Laid in the Tomb

Two men support the body of Jesus as it is lowered into the grave. One of the men is masked and dressed as a soldier. Two soldiers hold the body of Jesus between them. The scene follows the synoptic account of a quick burial without any anointings before the sabbath peace began. Jesus is shrouded loosely with a cloth around his midriff. The tomb is the common pit or hole in the ground, a detail that is not supported in the gospel account but that does reflect the typical crass disposal of the bodies of the crucified. The body of Jesus is already stiffened by the rigor of death.

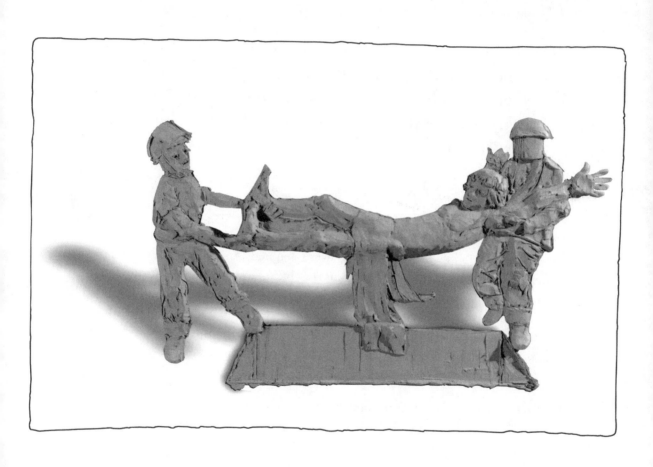

Blessed are you when people revile you and persecute you and utter all kinds of evil against you falsely on my account. Rejoice and be glad, for your reward is great in heaven, for in the same way they persecuted the prophets who were before you.
——Matthew 5:11-12

"Now there was a garden in the place where he was crucified, and in the garden there was a new tomb in which no one had ever been laid. And so, because it was the Jewish day of Preparation, and the tomb was nearby, they laid Jesus there" (Jn 19:41-42). Joseph of Arimathea laid the body "in his own new tomb, which he had hewn in the rock. He then rolled a great stone to the door of the tomb and went away. Mary Magdalene and the other Mary [the mother of James and Joses] were there, sitting opposite the tomb" (Mt 27:59-61). One thinks of the wisdom saying of Jesus: "new wine must be put into fresh wineskins" (Lk 5:38).

Jesus was born in the stable in Bethlehem "because there was no place for them in the inn" (Lk 2:7). In his death Jesus had no grave of his own. His homelessness speaks of this human life as a journey wherein none has a lasting city and everyone is nowhere at home. Jesus was homeless in Bethlehem and in danger for his life from King Herod. Put to death by Pontius Pilate, Jesus is yet homeless in death, and he is buried in someone else's tomb. "Foxes have holes, and birds of the air have nests; but the Son of Man has nowhere to lay his head" (Mt 8:20). Neither in life nor in death had he a place of his own. Jesus is a pilgrim of eternity, and his final and true home is with his Father who is in heaven.

The Father loved the Son, and God's love is never in vain. God will not be separated by death from whomever God loves. Those who love as God loves are loved by God. Nothing shall snatch them from God's hands. Death will be no more, for our God is a God of the living and not of the dead. The beloved of God will live. "O Lord my God, I cried to you for help, and you have healed me. O Lord, you brought up my soul from Sheol, restored me to life from among those gone down to the Pit" (Ps 30:2-3).

Nathaniel, one of the first disciples of Jesus, is invited to "come and see" where Jesus dwells in the kingdom of the living (Jn 1:46). When Lazarus is dead, Jesus asks where he is buried. His sister Mary answers, "Lord, come and see" and "Jesus began to weep" (Jn 11:34-35). He knows where we human beings do indeed dwell without him who is life. The kingdom of the dead is our last and final station on our own way of the cross. Death does not belong to Jesus. Nonetheless, Jesus must descend into the grave. He must descend even into hell. He goes down into the dark and the deep to wherever the dead must go. "They made his grave with the wicked and his tomb with the rich, although he had done no violence, and there was no deceit in his mouth" (Is

53:9). Jesus embraces that night, and God enlivens him and with him all of us. We emerge from out of the nothingness of death and into the plenitude of God's creation that lives forever. From the silence of the grave will rise a song of everlasting jubilation. With the burial of Jesus the Easter Vigil has begun. We watch and we wait with hope in our hearts. "For I know that my Redeemer lives" (Jb 19:25).

"Unless a grain of wheat falls into the earth and dies, it remains just a single grain; but if it dies, it bears much fruit" (Jn 12:24). The body of Jesus is sown in the ground of this world, and a new heaven and a new earth have begun. The stone womb will give birth to an everlasting life, stronger than the rock, a love stronger than death. The whole world is the expectant tomb, awaiting its quickening by God, who will raise his Son and the whole human cosmos along with him. "I consider that the sufferings of this present time are not worth comparing with the glory about to be revealed to us. For the creation waits with eager longing for the revealing of the children of God; for the creation was subjected to futility, not of its own will but by the will of the one who subjected it, in hope that the creation itself will be set free from its bondage to decay and will obtain the freedom of the glory of the children of God" (Rm 8:18-21). Samson pulled down the pillars; Joseph was delivered from the prison bars; Jonah was rescued from the belly of the whale; and Jesus Christ will not be held down by the "great stone" rolled to the entrance to seal his grave. "Where, O Death, is your sting?" (1 Cor 15:55).

Note

There would have been little time to bury Jesus before the sabbath peace began, and hence a gravesite nearby is presupposed. According to Matthew, Roman guards were stationed at the tomb site, lest the disciples steal the body of Jesus by night and claim that Jesus had risen from the dead (Mt 27:62-66). These details may reflect a much later controversy between Christians and Jews. That the tomb of Jesus was a new tomb in a garden may also be theological elaboration by the evangelists, who wished to teach how Jesus rose from the dead as the firstborn of a new creation. The exact order of events and the events' deepest meaning in faith are at times run together in the gospels.

In John's account, the body of Jesus is anointed with myrrh and aloes before he is buried (Jn 19:39). Indeed, Mary of Bethany anoints the feet of the living Jesus, who protests that she had done this "for the day of my burial" (Jn 12:1-8). In the other gospels, the implication is that there was no time to anoint the body of Jesus before the sunset that began the sabbath. Thus the women, who were present at the burial, go to the tomb on Sunday morning in order to anoint the body of Jesus. It is not clear how they were to roll back the stone. Perhaps none of the conflicting details of the anointing of the body of Jesus represents a known factual account. That the women find the tomb empty is recorded as the event that prompts the discovery of the mystery of the resurrection of Jesus Christ from the dead.

Just days ago
my heavy head
rested
on your welcome chest.
Hard with muscle
not with death.

Today with woe
and mother shed
tears, I'm tested
on your bone-still breast.
Open to gristle,
broken from beating,
finished with pleading
and begging for breath.

The three of us go
to lie you wed
to earth now grafted
may you rest.

Prayer

Jesus, martyr and king,

blessed be Joseph of Arimathea, who provided for you a tomb instead of a common grave with felons;

blessed be the ointment-bearing women who came to bathe, anoint, and shroud a body horrendous in appearance;

blessed be the new tomb that gave the Incarnate God a sabbath rest before he rose gloriously from the dead;

blessed be the angels who communicated to the faithful women the best news in the world;

blessed be God who brought us salvation through inward and outward suffering, through acute death, and through the resplendent, startling resurrection.
Amen.

Intercessions

Response: Jesus, invite us into your kingdom.

That we may see the grave as the earth where the seed is buried, dies, and is transformed:
    Jesus, invite us into your kingdom.

That funeral services may witness to us the vibrant hope of the resurrection:
    Jesus, invite us into your kingdom.

That we may not conduct our funerary rites with extravagance, but witness to Christian simplicity and hope:
    Jesus, invite us into your kingdom.

For the recovery of the remains of war and accident victims and consolation for their families:
    Jesus, invite us into your kingdom.

For cultures where wives must follow their spouses to the funeral pyre:
    Jesus, invite us into your kingdom.

Jesus Is Risen From the Dead

The grave in the ground is wide open, and the stone lid is thrown off to the side. One burial garment is cast to one side. A second piece of clothing is in the foreground, tossed aside casually in disregard for any inhibition of the resurrection glory. In the upper right background is a flourishing tree, a new "tree of life," rooted in the earth but reaching toward the heavens. Here the wood of the cross comes to a greening and to blossom, just as the seed once cast into the ground rises to new life.

> This is the day that the Lord has made;
> let us rejoice and be glad in it.
> ——Psalm 118:24

No one saw Jesus rise from the dead. We know only that the women found the tomb empty early on Sunday morning. One might well imagine that Jesus walked right through the rock. No one needed to open the grave for him to move. No one untied the winding burial sheet for Jesus. The cloth that covered his head was found "rolled up in a place by itself" (Jn 20:7). The stone was rolled back so that the women could see the body was not there, and the angels told them he is risen. A week later Jesus suddenly stood in the midst of his disciples even though the doors of the house were locked (Jn 20:19). Jesus rose to a new bodily life. He did not come back to this life as we know it. Unlike Lazarus, who rose resuscitated from the dead and who would die again, Jesus overcame death. He will never die again. His body and soul have become transfigured, and his life in the body walks in the eternal life of the kingdom of God.

Birthing into this life has transformed everything. Jesus was born into eternity with the same unique scars of this life, but now wounds made glorious. And so shall we, who are brother and sister to him. We are one body with Jesus risen from the dead. Here is the garden of the new creation. This is the new day of the new world. Here is the human body as it was never known before, a body without any shadow of death. "See, the home of God is among mortals. He will dwell with them as their God; they will be his people, and God himself will be with them; he will wipe every tear from their eyes. Death will be no more; mourning and crying and pain will be no more, for the first things have passed away" (Rev 21:3-4). Crucified between thieves, Jesus rose from the grave between the tombs of the dead of all times and all places. "Listen, I will tell you a mystery! We will not all die, but we will all be changed, in a moment, in the twinkling of an eye, at the last trumpet. For the trumpet will sound, and the dead will be raised imperishable, and we will be changed" (1 Cor 15:51-52).

Note

It is important to note that the women reported to be at the foot of the cross were also witnesses to the burial. It is crucial that on Easter morning the discovery of the empty tomb is the discovery of the tomb of Jesus. The burial was not beneath the ground but in a cave carved out of the rock. A large rock was rolled to the entrance of the tomb to protect the body from wild animals.

The stone can, however, be moved with effort. One might remember the tomb of Lazarus, where Jesus gives orders that the stone be rolled back and with a command calls Lazarus forth from the dead, even though it has been four days and he remained bound hand and foot in burial shrouds (Jn 11).

To be conscious of everything in the cosmos
And to be a child with little of the past and a vague future,
And not knowing the meaning or where love is secure,
Is to be human.

To have no control over one's beginnings
And none over the endings of our lives,
And not much in between,
Is to be human.

Any revelation of why or wherefore would save us,
And the promise of a kingdom of God enliven us.
Good Friday is the human condition;
Easter Sunday the revelation.
Christ is risen, truly he is risen.
And now we know; God loves us dearly.

Prayer

Jesus, you tarried in the snug tomb for three days.
    You rolled away the stone
        to open a new age to the world.
Your kingdom *has come* through your glorification.
Help us to conceive beyond your individual resurrection
    to a new potential
        for all humanity
           for all creatures
             and for our mother earth.
Bathe our planet in the rays of the Sun of Righteousness.
    Engender a new paradise on earth
        rooted in justice and peace
           because Jesus Christ is present eternally.
             Amen.

Inscrutable Trinity,
    we have walked through the valley of the shadow of death
        into the lightshod realms of eternal life.
            Grant that, after our death,
                we may see you face-to-face
                and know you,
                        even as we are known.
            Amen.

Bibliography

Shantz. Susan D. *The Stations of the Cross: A Calculated Trap?* London, Ontario: Centre for Social and Humanistic Studies, University of Western Ontario, 1991.

Storme, Albert. *The Way of the Cross: A Historical Sketch.* Jerusalem: Franciscan Printing Press, 1976.

Thurston, Herbert. *The Stations of the Cross: An Account of Their History and Devotional Purpose.* London: Burns and Oates, 1906.

Works Cited

De Vinck, Catherine. *News of the World in Fifteen Stations*. Allendale, N.J.: Alleluia Press, 1988.

McAnally, Mary and Normal Dolph. *Stations: Paintings and Poems of the Spiritual Journey*. St. Paul, Minnesota: Pemmican/Open Door, 1995.

Nouwen, Henri. *Walk with Jesus: Stations of the Cross*. Maryknoll, N.Y.: Orbis Books, 1990.

Notes

1. It is worth noting that, even today, the stations of the cross are in some places chosen differently. For example, Pope John Paul II has for many years followed a *via crucis* more closely aligned with the biblical witness, with stations beginning at the Last Supper and the Garden of Gethsemane and following the notable events in the passion accounts in the four gospels.
2. See 2 Maccabees 7.
3. These women appear to be professional mourners. They were wise women who composed melodies and poetry for the occasion.
4. A detail furnished by Josephus, a contemporary Jewish historian.
5. Martin Buber.
6. Hebrews 12:1-3.
7. William Shakespeare.
8. 1 Samuel 16:7.

About the Authors:

Nicholas Ayo is a priest and member of the Congregation of Holy Cross, for whom he has served as novice director. A scholar of literature and theology, Fr. Ayo teaches in the Program of Liberal Studies at the University of Notre Dame and has authored several books, including *The Hail Mary: A Verbal Icon of Mary* and *The Lord's Prayer: A Survey Theological and Literary.*

James Flanigan, also a Holy Cross priest, is an artist who draws as well as sculpting in metal and clay.

Joseph Ross is a published poet and prison chaplain, working with death row inmates. He, too, is a priest and member of the Congregation of Holy Cross.

J. Massyngbaerde Ford is a biblical scholar and spiritual teacher. A professor of theology at the University of Notre Dame, she has authored a number of books, including *Welcoming Heaven: Prayers and Reflections for the Dying and Those Who Love Them.*